Truth-Prints

Also by Suzanne Ironbiter

POETRY

Devi

Devi: Mother of My Mind

How Fish Learn

The Ideal in the Mind

FICTION

The Secret Journey of Issa

Truth-Prints

Of Books and Teachers

Essays and Poems 2021-2025

Suzanne Ironbiter

Owlfeather Collective

Published by Owlfeather Collective
www.owlfeather.net

ISBN 978-0-9976218-5-3

Book design by Catherine Ednie

For my daughters and grandchildren

Table of Contents

Thoth said, "This discipline of writing, oh King, will make the Egyptians wiser and improve their memories. I have invented a prescription for memory and wisdom."

The King said, "Out of fondness for your offspring, you have attributed to writing the opposite of its real power. This discovery will produce forgetfulness in the souls of those who have learned it. Instead of their inner resources, they will rely on writing to bring things to their remembrance through external signs. What you have discovered ... will furnish your pupils with opinion, not true wisdom."

—Socrates reporting to Phaedrus in Plato, *Phaedrus* 275a (370 BCE)

"there's nothing to grab in the wellspring of truth
the world keeps chasing footprints of falsehood"
I wish I could fathom these ancient words

—from "Reading Zen Texts in the Morning at Transcendent Master Temple" by Liu Zongyang (805), translated by Red Pine (1993)

The very concept of truth is fading out of this world.
This prospect frightens me more than bombs.

—George Orwell's diary, read in Raoul Peck's 2025 documentary *Orwell: 2+2=5*

Waves

like waves by the shore

thoughts arise

go for a roll

subside

arise

go for a roll

sometimes one catches a ride

Dark Forests

Theodore Rousseau's painting "The Forest in Winter at Sunset" is very large (64" x 102 3/8") and very dark. He worked on it from 1846, when he was 34, to 1867, when he died at 55 without having accounted it as finished. At the Met Museum it hangs amidst smaller, brighter, more colorful paintings by him and other Barbizon artists. Its darkness makes it easy to pass by. Instead, one can sit on a bench in front of it and slowly become accustomed to the darkness the way eyes become accustomed to the darkness in a room. Pupils dilate, retinal cones give way to rods, color and detail fade, focus wanders seeking clarity.

For some reason I couldn't understand, after I sat with this painting, it stayed in my mind for several weeks, like a dream I couldn't interpret. Why did it feel so personally meaningful?

The forest towers over, shades, and renders almost invisible two small human figures. They do not seem to be on any path out of the woods as night closes in. In the larger perspective of Rousseau seeing and sketching this scene in plein air, did they just happen to be there? Did he put them there with a purpose? (I later saw, in a book, a charcoal drawing of this scene in which they do not appear.) I began to feel I was one of them. This forest seemed not unlike those in the Hudson Valley where I live and walk amongst trees.

On the Met website, I read that Rousseau was a lover and protector of trees and of nature. He was intent on observing and rendering the nuances of light and season and the personalities of individual trees, particularly great oaks. At his and his fellow Barbizon painters' request, the Forest of Fontainebleau, where he experienced this sunset, became the world's first protected nature preserve in 1853. Alfred Sensier, friend and biographer of both Rousseau and Rousseau's friend Millet, wrote, "the proud majesty of the old trees, the virgin state of rocks and heath...all these intoxicated them with their beauty and their smell. They were, in truth, possessed." I could feel how his intoxication, its emotional tone and mood, energized this painting as he worked on it over so many years.

At the library I found Steven Adams's *The Barbizon School and the Origins of Impressionism* (1994). Theophile Thore was one of the first critics to appreciate Barbizon paintings as a record both of natural landscapes and of the insight of the artists' poetic, subjective vision. Thore saw them as an antidote to the venal materialism of modern life, for which I agree that we need antidotes. He especially singled out Rousseau's art and practice of sustained looking. He described Rousseau's eyes as "fixed and voracious," with images of Fontainebleau "passing before the vault of the artist's eyebrows." Rather than doing various preparatory studies, Rousseau often worked on his paintings for years, comparing this process "with an image emerging from the mist, or the process of creation itself."

Unlike most artists, he painted in the forest year-round. The forest's seclusion corresponded to his alienation from the Salon. I too feel alienated from the market mainstream. Sensier described him "alone with his forest, carried off by a whirlwind of sensations in which he loved to savour the rugged landscape or the imposing silence of the forest." Thore warned him of the risk of his prolonged separations from society.

Jean Bouret's *The Barbizon School* (1973) quotes from a letter Rousseau wrote to Sensier. "The human soul is like the forest where we walk, plundered at will by evil woodsmen; the flowering plants are stifled; the high timber of our thoughts is felled; the new shoots in quest of the sun are cut back; the proud rocks of our will are splintered and reduced to dust; the highlands that rise to the skies are flattened and when the essential nature of everything is utterly distorted, all-pervasive rank weeds, without form, without spirit and without colour, are sown in the debris of the soul." More than a century and a half later, how much more does it feel that this is the case!

One of the Rousseau paintings reproduced in Adams's book, "Under the Beech Trees, Evening (The Parish Priest)," from 1842-3, has a very small dark figure of a priest seated, as if in contemplation, on the ground under a small stand of tall slender-trunked beech trees, his position a counterpart, in centricity and obscurity, to the two figures in "The Forest in Winter." Adams writes about the effect of Rousseau's method of composition and focus on the spectator's attention, requiring the sustained looking that he practiced.

My continuing effort to penetrate Rousseau's painted darkness virtualized on a laptop screen reminds me of my effort to look into "Anangon Kekenimad," a very dark 2022 painting by Tom Uttech that I had seen at Alexandre Gallery. Uttech's paintings are set in the watery Northwoods of my home state of Wisconsin and neighboring Minnesota, a world Uttech loves, the homeland of the Ojibway people, whose language provides his titles. This painting is small, only 31" x 39", and completely nocturnal, well past sunset. Between the dark silhouettes of winter trees on either side, the silhouette of an erect bear stands on a tuft of dark ground beside a lake with a distant wooded shore, all hard to see. The sky and reflecting lake are deep bluish gray. They are dotted with tiny pinpoints of stars, almost invisible. It's hard to make out, but I think the bear is looking at the lake and the stars, his back turned toward us. I may be wrong. Usually in Uttech's paintings the bear is looking at us.

In an artist's statement, Uttech writes, "My painting is an attempt to share the state of mind I can enter when alone in the Northwoods... This environment affects me most strongly in the crepuscular light of dawn and dusk. When I am there at this time of day, and with a clean and empty mind, a door opens for me to enter a state of tranquil ecstasy." His hope is that viewers will be affected by the scene and his response, "that they will accept the myriad interconnectedness and adjust their lives accordingly."

In her essay, "Tom Uttech: Magnetic North," Lucy R. Lippard points out that Uttech is "of German ancestry, heir to the spirituality of the Protestant north" with its romantic feeling for the presence of spirit in nature, part of my own heritage. This sense of spiritual presence also connects with Native American ways of seeing.

The catalogue for the 2022 Uttech show includes poetry by Kimberly Blaeser, an Ojibway woman poet. There is an introductory essay, "Surface, Depth, and Communion," on the "Indigenous sense of the sacred...just below the surface of his brush strokes," by the Kiowa writer N. Scott Momaday. One of Blaeser's poems concludes: "Like amphibians in winter we, too, sink deep / patient as sphagnum moss–wait, for return."

A sense of return, of surface, depth, and communion underlies the spiritual dimension interwoven with the physical dimension in nature and in Uttech's paintings. Often animals are either looking at us or fleeing from right to left through the forest, as if alerting us to or escaping from some urgent danger. In Rousseau's painting too, the hidden eyes of the forest seem to be watching us, like the arboreal community of interconnected awareness, including awareness of danger, the forester Peter Wohlleben describes in *The Hidden Life of Trees* (2016).

Although I had found so many points of personal rapport with both of these dark forest paintings, I still felt there was some kind of symbolic interpretation eluding me. I suspected that it had to do with my entering the dark night and winter season of my life, a time requiring patience. Furthermore, my liberal cultural values, along with the interdisciplinary cross-cultural humanities that I had studied and taught and continued to value, are in a dark winter season, their supporting institutions endangered globally like forests and trees.

When I retired from teaching in 2022, in addition to my longtime spiritual practice of writing poetry, I began writing personal essays reflecting on things I found worthwhile to think and learn about. In preparation for publishing an octogenarian collection for my 85th birthday, I gave the manuscript to my friend Catherine to edit. When I received her comments and saw how thoughtfully and insightfully she had journeyed through the clearings, trails, and dense thickets of my text, I realized that the collection was my forest in winter at sunset and she had joined me there as a companion. She wrote that she experienced the book as, among other things, "a manual for aging." Thank you, dear Catherine!

I first sat on the bench in front of the Rousseau painting with my friend Dennis, who introduced me to the Barbizon painters and to the practice of personal essay writing. He helpfully read each of the essays as they emerged over the last three years. My daughter Anna read through the first draft of the collection, made good suggestions, and encouraged me to proceed. Thank you, dear Anna and Dennis!

Winter Birds

As I, sealed indoors,
sat overwhelmed seeing the white
depths of snow crystals fallen
through deep cold for a day and a night
from the far sunless sky,

outside my window there arrived
a small flock of juncos,
their back coats softly toned
to the grays of bare branches,
their breasts to the pale sky.

They nibbled seeds from the feeder,
hopped on mounds of snow,
puffed their plumage,
and perched on tall boughs,
not at all overwhelmed.

Chickadees, sparrows, woodpeckers,
finches, titmice, and nuthatches
came by one by one,
so lovely their feathers keeping
so warm their hearts.

Is it that I, sealed in my body
as age deepens its hold
in the winter of my days,
have atrophied mind's
wings of freedom?

Transience

At this moment in April 2021, I find myself reading W.G. Sebald's 1998 essay on Johann Peter Hebel (1760-1826), a Lutheran theologian known as the Housefriend for his stories in almanacs.

Like Sebald, he was from the Alemannic region where my grandma was born. His stories connect, in a folksy, non-theological way, the universe, the household, natural history, and the soul.

Sebald surmises that Hebel sensed in 1812/13, toward the end of the Napoleonic wars, "that history, from that point on, would amount to nothing other than the martyrologium of mankind."

In Hebel's poem "Transience," a rustic father and son journey to Basel in an oxcart by night. The son sees a ruined castle–it looks, he says, like Death in a Dance of the Dead--and asks if such ruin can befall their house. The father says, "Yes, all things come to an end."

If he is good, the father adds, the boy will go to a distant star and there they will meet again. They will see, from the Milky Way, the Earth in ruins. (This was written circa 1800.)

The father describes the distant stars as shining villages. A beautiful city lies hidden in the Milky Way.

In the late 1950s, canoeing in the northern Wisconsin and Minnesota lake country sacred to the Ojibway, I camped under the spectacle of stars telling their stories.

Because of light pollution, it's hard to see "the floor of heaven / ...inlaid with patens of bright gold" as I did then.

The Perseverance rover and Ingenuity helicopter have landed with a camera on Mars, a planet named for the god of war, perhaps to discover if something there came to a violent end, or if some of us humans can escape to there, having brought ruin to Earth.

Mineral extraction and pollution threaten the health and beauty of the northern lakes and rivers. Huge ocean boats and cruise ships penetrate the Great Lakes all the way from the Atlantic to the west shore of Lake Superior.

On YouTube I heard a young Ojibway water protector, Autumn Peltier, tell of her people's journey by canoe from the salt sea through the Great Lakes. A bright shell guided them to their sacred food, *manoomin,* wild rice that still grows in the Minnesota lake country and that my Ojibway grandson has harvested there.

Autumn describes how she perceives the thoughts and feelings of water through our experience in womb waters, our being more than half water, and how our woman side tunes to water.

Carole Lindstrom (Ojibway) and Michaela Goade (Tlingit) have made an award-winning children's book, *We Are Water Protectors* (2020), about Indigenous women as water protectors. It begins, "Water is the first medicine."

On a pilgrimage with my Ojibway grandchildren to Lake Michigan's Whitefish Bay near where I was born, I wept as I felt my emotions of loss cresting and settling in the waters.

My grandchildren gathered, as I used to do, stones smoothed by the waves, stones shining when wet.

Wisconsin Flowage

Maybe what I am remembering is the flow and feel of the waters
around my canoe and my body, around the bodies of loons and of fishes
as ospreys seized them into air, the continua of light and sound
from the waters' ripples to the aspens' quiver,
gleams and shadows on white birch, a deer almost unseen,
her coat dappled as she drinks by the water's edge,
all of this moved by the flows of rivers, lakes, and creeks, of winds and breaths
in which the same never reappears. One can never reenter it.
One could not even ever again be where one was for a moment.
Amidst these vast acres of water, the mind in its canoe found its way
from day to day, camping at night by a stream. Overhead, the flowages of stars.

I seem to remember, too, or did I imagine it, a small, quiet lake, a mirror to the sky,
its refreshment from earth-rooted springs, a mother's hands, wrapping my body.
I cannot say that I was cleansed or reborn. I was where I was for a moment.

More than sixty years ago it was, when I was young, that I entered this flowage.
It reminded me, even then, it seemed, of something I needed to remember.

Books, Seeds, and Stars

1.

My graduate school mentor was Paul Oskar Kristeller, a scholar devoted to the recovery, survival, and study of endangered ancient, medieval, and renaissance texts and manuscripts.

Of Jewish descent, having fled Hitler's Germany in 1933 and then Mussolini's Italy in 1939, he had a lived sense of the endangerment of books and the fragility of civilizations.

It was something that he communicated not so much in words but in his demeanor, his quietly intense and patient honoring of all that he studied.

During the 1968 student protests at Columbia our seminar met in his apartment on West 120th Street. I remember him sitting beside a table covered with an oriental rug, his cat on his lap, continuing from wherever it was we had left off.

In the mid-nineties, after more than twenty years of my not pursuing the scholarly work for which I had been trained, I read an essay by him lamenting the decline of academic humanities.

I wrote him a letter saying how much I appreciated studying with him, how although I had ended up abandoning Greek and Latin for Sanskrit and Indian philosophy, he remained a deep and treasured influence on my academic values and commitment to text-based study and teaching.

He thanked me for my note. Although he appreciated the path I had taken, he wrote, he did not see a hopeful future in his lifetime.

He was ninety then and passed away in his home four years later.

I find myself thinking of him today as I endeavor to read ancient Greek lyric poets.

Their work exists mostly in fragments quoted in other texts or in bits from crumbled papyri unearthed by archeologists, as did the writings of the pre-Socratic philosophers we studied in one of his seminars.

The unearthed fragments have been described as the size of large corn flakes.

It's hard to imagine the patience of scholars as they put together these shreds of thought with the weight of feathers, seeds, or pollen from a past so long gone.

And yet sometimes an ancient word or phrase will seem so beautiful that its sound is like a mantra dropping a plumbline through time, or like a star from unfathomable light-years ago only visible to us now.

2.

The Sanskrit adjective *guru* means heavy. It is cognate with Greek *barus*, Latin *gravis*.

A guru carries the pregnant weight of old knowledge to be reborn in new students.

Traditionally sitting on the ground in a well-balanced posture, he sinks from his head into his breath and his body, yoking and aligning thought, speech, and physical presence.

My first teacher of yoga meditation and Sanskrit was Acharya Sushil Kumar, a Jain guru.

Jains picture their heart, seat of mind, as a luminous diamond on which, over many lifetimes, painful residues of karma accrue like heavy tar.

Harmful acts, words, and thoughts generate the most pain-causing deposits.

Through non-violent discipline and meditation, Jain enlightened ones burn the tar from their hearts.

They become clear and bright like guiding stars.

Guruji taught us mantras for purifying our mind and our body, for seeing and hearing hidden connections through sounds and letters.

In a world full of conflict, his teaching was dedicated to religious harmony, peace, and non-violence.

He is long gone from his body. I still chant the mantras. I still treasure his book *Song of the Soul: An Introduction to the Science of Sound* (1987). My meditation posture is now in a chair.

When I met Guruji in the early 1970s I had just completed my PhD with an intellectual focus on pre-modern western mystical philosophies.

My husband and I were academics accustomed to carrying heavy loads of books back and forth from the entrails of university libraries, like a purgatorial burden on our journey from ignorance toward a remote aspiration of wisdom.

Guruji came to the yoga studio in the woods on Upper Shad Road in Pound Ridge, north of New York City, where we were learning to experience a slowed-down non-dual view of the mind and the body.

During graduate school I repeatedly had a dream of being in a desert at the base of a cliff shelved with books.

When I finished my dissertation, I dreamed myself scaling the book wall and running out of the desert.

Over the years, our house in the woods filled with books.

I had dreams of crypt-like spaces where I was seeking some imagined book hidden away long ago like a message in a bottle at sea.

By then I was a mother and had come to know the pregnant meaning of heaviness.

In another dream, the spirit of my deceased paternal grandmother gave me two flowers, a pledge of two daughters.

A serious gardener and keeper of seeds, she kept a Garden Club book full of poems such as W. D. Woodward's "Resurrection" about the autumnal gayness of leaves: "When leaves go into mourning / For the dying of the year, / They never clothe themselves in black, / Nor sorrowful appear."

When my father was near death, she appeared to him, lighting his way to the other side.

Sometimes in dreams she gave me a book in a script I could read only in dreams, like the way scripts appear hidden in the textures of tree barks or the changing surface of water or murmuring along under the surface of thought.

In the early 2010s, as old age and solitary widowhood weighed upon me, while the perils of the Anthropocene multiplied year by year upon our descendants, Khenpo Karthar Rinpoche, abbot of Karma Triyana Dharmachakra center in Woodstock, New York, became my guru.

Born in 1924, he was among those who had escaped from Tibet in 1958 after the Chinese takeover of their country.

I felt blessed to have found an elder with a wisdom both scholarly and manifest in his person.

He gave empowerments involving seed mantras and seeds of light, and teachings wherein we received his transmission of classic texts.

This is called a warm or breathed transmission, conveying intimately realized meaning and awareness into this living moment.

Tibetan texts for teachings and liturgies for empowerments are block-printed in loose oblong folios, tied between wooden covers, and wrapped in cloth, with a cloth label at one end.

Khenpo Karthar would unwrap the book and read through it with comments. At intervals he paused for the translator to render his reading and commentary into English.

Refugees leaving Tibet carried out thousands of these texts.

In 1999 the Tibetan Buddhist Research Center was founded to acquire, preserve, scan, digitize, and make available a twelve thousand volume treasury of endangered Tibetan texts.

Rooms lined with shelves of Tibetan books, with their sunny yellow, orange, white, or red cloths and labels, have a wonderful warm fragrance.

Every morning I unwrap and read the liturgies of my empowered practices.

In 2019, when Rinpoche left his body, we were invited to mix our mind with his and to read the liturgy for calling the guru from afar.

3.

The Tall Book of Mother Goose is the first book I remember from when I was very young.

My mother read me the poems page by page. I memorized all the verses and can still recite most of them.

Here perhaps began my taste for esoteric meanings about which I had no clue.

(Many nursery rhymes, I later learned, satirize historical dramas. For example, absurd efforts to avoid a royal imposition are behind "three wise men of Gotham went to sea in a bowl–if the bowl had been stronger, my tale had been longer.")

Some of the verses have words of wisdom. "A wise old owl sat in an oak, the more he saw the less he spoke, the less he spoke the more he heard–why don't you follow that wise old bird?"

I advanced from these delights to Edward Lear's limericks and poems, such as "The Owl and the Pussycat" and "The Dong with the Luminous Nose," the poems in *Alice in Wonderland,* and Robert Louis Stevenson's *A Child's Garden of Verses.* I memorized these poems too and can still recite some of them.

It's always uplifting to hear how the owl and the pussycat "dined on mince, and slices of quince, / Which they ate with a runcible spoon; / And hand in hand, on the edge of the sand, / They danced by the light of the moon, / The moon, / The moon, / They danced by the light of the moon."

Then there were the Wesleyan hymns, like "Love divine, all loves excelling," and the rhythms of psalms and liturgy recited in the Methodist church, where my family went every Sunday.

My childhood home had a small bookshelf with adult books including two poetry anthologies: *The Chief American Poets* (1905) and *The World's Best Poems* (1929).

In the American poetry anthology my mother had written her name and address when she was a student at the University of Michigan in Ann Arbor. She had marked poems in the contents as if they were assigned in class, and there are occasional markings throughout the book, which includes poems by Emerson, Whittier, Lowell, Lanier, Whitman, Longfellow, and Poe. No Dickinson appears.

Beginning when I was perhaps nine years old, when we lived in Boston in the historic environment of some of these poets, I loved dipping into this book. I particularly enjoyed the Longfellow poems. They slipped into my memory. "There is a quiet spirit in these woods./ ...With what a tender and impassioned voice/ it fills the nice and delicate ear of thought..."

As I look through the books I still have from the house where I grew up, I find also a 1908 book of James Whitcomb Riley's *Child-Rhymes* which must have been given to my mother as a child, my mother's old Bible, an 1891 *Golden Treasury of the Best Songs and Lyrics in the English Language,* and a 1907 poetic wisdom compilation, *Life's Common Way,* which must have belonged to my maternal grandma. The lines "'Careful with fire' is good advice, we know;/ 'careful with words' is ten times doubly so" are underlined. There is also a 1927 book of *India's Love Lyrics* and a very small old prayer book, *Key of Heaven,* given to my paternal grandfather by his mother for Christmas in 1899, when he was seventeen years old.

Although I was born in 1941, when the seeds of modernism were at large, I was curiously implanted in my youth with Victorian poetry and spirituality and an undercurrent of German romantic idealism. I keep the old books archived as if in a bank of endangered seeds.

4.

My thoughts about the weight of books and teachers arose from reading about the German artist Anselm Kiefer after seeing *Anselm,* Wim Wenders's 2023 documentary about him.

I have been moved by Kiefer's work since it began to appear in gallery and museum exhibits in and around New York City.

His images draw from the kind of esoteric and poetic books I have in my library. Also, he is from the area of southwestern Germany where I have studied and where my maternal grandma was born.

His paintings from 1969 to 1991 addressed Germany and the horrors of World War II lest they be forgotten.

In the late 1980s he set aside his painter's palette to sculpt a library of two hundred volumes, their pages made of lead.

He bought lead taken down from the roof of Köln cathedral during its restoration.

Though heavy, lead is fluid like water. It is the primary matter alchemy turns into gold. It corresponds with the melancholy of Saturn and the melancholy of artists, Saturn's children.

Some pages in the library are marked with paint, clay, or glued-on photos, hair, and ash.

Some pages are empty except for having been weathered and run over outdoors.

As if recovered from a mythic realm before history began, a time of giants, the books are shelved on two huge steel racks.

The title of the sculpture, "Land of Two Rivers–the High Priestess," evokes the long-ago cultures of Fertile Crescent and Nile.

The Tarot High Priestess guards the sacred knowledge recorded by Thoth, the divine Egyptian scribe, aka Hermes.

In *Phaedrus,* Socrates recounts the legend that the Egyptian King Thamus rejected Thoth's gift of writing because "it will implant forgetfulness in men's souls."

Kiefer says, "I make my own books to find my own way through the old stories."

For several years Kiefer crafted heavy libraries—lead pages without writing, without words—with esoteric titles evoking lost Hermetic and Kabbalistic wisdom.

For example, "The Breaking of the Vessels," thirty lead books on a steel bookcase with ribbons of lead, broken glass, and copper wire, references the 16th-century Spanish Kabbalist Isaac Luria's myth of creation.

To make a space for the world, God withdrew into himself. He reentered the empty space as light and emanated ten vessels to hold the light. The last seven vessels shattered from the force of the light. Partially through human work, the lost light is in a process of being raised back toward God. This is our human purpose.

Kiefer says, "The work in its failure—and it will always fail—will still illuminate."

Beginning in 1995, Kiefer made portraits of himself lying naked on the ground in *shavasana,* the yoga corpse pose. It's interesting that he chooses this pose, suitable for resting from work or from life, not the sitting meditation pose, suited for burning tar from the heart.

In one portrait, "Sol Invictus," he is being showered with seeds falling from the face of a tall dry sunflower high above him, its face watching over him, its leaves lowered close to its stem like closed wings.

The black seeds, tumbling out and down, fill the air and lie thick on the ground above his head and on his upper chest, covering his heart.

In another painting, "The Rose Gives Honey to the Bees," he lies in the center of the canvas. In corpse pose, now wearing white yoga pants, suspended as if levitating, he is encircled by bits of honeycomb and sunseeds.

In "For Robert Fludd," a 17-page cardboard book honoring the 17th-century Hermeticist, photos show the life cycle of sunflowers in a field. When the seed-studded flowers ripen and turn black, they become stars, corresponding heaven and earth.

"The Secret Life of Plants" is a 13-page cardboard book of photos and sunflowers mapped in relation to patterns of stars. The title is from a 1972 book exploring through modern science the intelligence of plants and living cells, their communication with the astral energies of the universe as they were intuited by ancient mystical philosophies.

That theme continues in a lead book more than six feet high, standing upright like a person, its open pages bending under their own weight. Stars, their NASA ID numbers, and lines connecting them are drawn on the dark pages—stars we can no longer see because of our light pollution, another residue of our collective karma.

As I write now, it is 2024 and I am eighty-three, four years older than Kiefer. Many of my friends, like Kiefer, struggle to find shards of light. The darkness of our environmental violence and polarized humanity thickens every day.

When I turned seventy, I took refuge and began my immersion in Buddhist reading, reflection and writing. I added it to my previous practice of yoga study and meditation. Without daily spiritual practice, I could not bear the darkness. For me, it is a practical, not a metaphysical requirement.

For her ninetieth year, my friend Judith, a retired trauma therapist, dedicated herself to a year of Torah study through a weekly cycle of readings, reflection, and writing. She had recently moved from my neighborhood to a senior living apartment in New Hampshire. Poetry, meditation, archetypal work, and spiritual teachings had always been part of her daily life. She began her immersion in Torah when she turned seventy. Her book *Blessing from Broken* records week by week how Torah study guided her "in going forth...to lift up the broken pieces of my life and those of my ancestors and those of the world" in her ninetieth year.

My friend Hans, now a nonagenarian, has for some years taken *A Course in Miracles* as his daily spiritual practice. He is a retired Presbyterian pastor and on-going activist in prisoner and poverty reform.

My most aged friend Betty is well into her nineties. She is losing her vision, hearing, and mobility, yet she has not lost her radiant smile or her lifelong commitment to prayer. She leads a local prayer chain, calling us to pray for whomever she has heard is in difficulties.

I have much to learn from these three, my most elderly living friends, their faces bright with love and kindness, as I gather mental reinforcement amidst the challenges of old age.

Blessings

Outside of my window
a lowering sun draws to its touch
long fingers of goldenrod.
Linden boughs clothed in gold
bend toward day's going down
as if praying before sleep.

Inside of my window
on my fourscore years
night casts its shadow.
I feel the tender oldness of friends—

the brow of my teacher, nearing 100,
pressing my brow;
the hands of my friend's mother, nearing 100,
fluttering into mine like small birds left behind,
unsure why they have not yet flown away;
the hands of my friend, over 90, her sight dimmed,
all her life praying for others, requesting others' prayers;
the hands of my friend, nearing 90,
reassuring me with his touch
that death is not, as he had supposed all his life,
to be feared, that the Kingdom of God is administered
with grace and with miracle, unlike that of man.

Precepts

1.

I love it when the three boys in *The Magic Flute* instruct Tamino and Papageno to "be steadfast, patient, and discreet!"

My parents initiated me into proverbial culture by repeating old saws such as "a stitch in time saves nine," "you never can tell the depth of the well by the length of the handle on the pump," and "a bird in the hand is worth two in the bush."

They sent me to Methodist Church School where we learned the Golden Rule, the Great Commandment, and the Ten Commandments.

From about the ages of eight to eighteen, I was a serious girl scout with the motto "Be Prepared." (This was in the 1950s in Milwaukee.)

There was also a scout slogan, "Do a good turn daily."

I recited a pledge involving the Girl Scout Law, a law which I must have memorized but have to look up now. My honor was to be trusted, my duty was to be useful and help others, I was to be loyal, courteous, a friend to all and a sister to every other girl scout no matter to what social class she belonged. I was to keep myself pure, be a friend to animals, obey orders, and be cheerful and thrifty.

I guess I liked having guidelines. There was also an incentive to knowledge, as all sorts of badges could be earned, and I did that assiduously.

(For scouts today, they've added improving the world and wise use of resources. Loyalty, courtesy, purity, cheer, and thrift have been exchanged for considerateness, courage, strength, respect of authority, respect of self and others, and responsibility.)

In elementary school we also pledged allegiance to the flag of a nation "with liberty and justice for all." (We did not back then say "under God.")

In the sixties, when I was a student coming into adulthood, respect for authority and obedience evaporated in the context of racial injustice, the Vietnam War, and environmental issues. Civic-mindedness became more oppositional.

I vowed the marital vow "to love and to cherish" and obeyed the first commandment, "Be fruitful and multiply."

My husband and I took up yoga meditation with the motto "may there be peace in the world, and may it begin with me," with non-violence as the first rule.

In the nineties, my husband died of a heart attack. Our daughter was fruitful and multiplied. The new family moved in with me.

The father got drunk, squandered money, fooled around, and did not follow precepts.

I was not prepared.

To get a handle on the situation, I attended a Buddhist meditation retreat involving ten days without speech, reading, or writing.

Every evening we heard a dharma talk by the teacher, Mr. Goenka.

His message could be summed up in these words: "See things as they are, not as you want them to be."

Thoughts and emotions arise, they pass away, they arise, they pass away. Disturbing things come and go, anger comes and goes. Calmness arises, passes away, and begins to abide longer.

With a voice like a dragon in a Himalayan cave, Mr. Goenka chanted Buddhist dohas in Hindi at the end of meditation sessions.

From Day Two, here's one in translation: "May I and may the world be free from agitation. This is the art of living, this is pure Dhamma."

Here's another, from Day Ten: "May ripples of love spread through the pool of the mind. May every pore give forth the sound, 'May all beings be happy!'"

Each chant sequence ended with "May all beings be happy!"

Day Ten is the day of maitri, friendship, loving-kindness, when silence is broken and participants share their experiences.

Practices having been introduced and established, reading is now allowed.

In Mr. Goenka's pamphlet, *The Art of Living: Vipassana Meditation,* we read that Buddha established an art of living, not a religion. He taught his students "to observe nature as it is, by observing the reality inside."

With Vipassana practice, calming the mind and observing its transient stream, words flow by, precepts flow by, judgments flow by, emotions flow by.

Maitri, like the Golden Rule, abides as truth, as Dharma.

Vipassana trains the mind to deal, emotionally and practically, with things that are not as we want them to be.

It's a practice, not a precept. My appreciation expanded from precepts to practice.

2.

After around twenty years of being a student and more than fifty years of teaching, I retired. Nevertheless I stayed attached to the annual school/study routine.

For the first semester of retirement, in pursuit of pithy moral insights, I gave myself a course on Spinoza's *Ethics*.

I got the Latin text along with various commentaries.

Spinoza's patient, methodical, geometrical discipline of Definitions, Explanations, Axioms, Lemmas, Propositions, Proofs, Corollaries, and Scholia relaxed my mind by going mostly over my head.

I told myself that the geometrical style was an artistic expression of his argument that extension and thought are inseparable attributes of one substance, of nature, of the way things are.

I liked Rebecca Goldstein's argument, in *Betraying Spinoza* (2006), that his ordering of thought slows time down, that it is a rejection of the Biblical focus on divine historicity, and that he did it in the context of 17th-century chaos, when historical changes were accelerating as they are now.

I liked Clare Carlisle's argument, in *Spinoza's Religion* (2021), that I was joining a community of readers much like Spinoza's circle of readers, "sharing in the same reflexive intellectual activity," including calling to mind previous statements and appreciating "the human goods of intellectual striving and intellectual rest or repose."

This seemed especially nice since I was concerned about feeling isolated without students and colleagues.

I was impressed by Spinoza's application to ecology today. He was arguing against Descartes's mind-body separation, its dualistic tendency to exploit and alienate the physical.

"The object of the idea that constitutes a human mind is a body, or a specific actually existing mode of extension, and nothing else." (II.13) "...the whole of nature is one individual thing, whose parts, i.e. all bodies, vary in an infinite number of ways without any change to the whole individual..." (II.13.L7, Scholium)

In *Looking for Spinoza* (2003), the neurophysiologist Antonio Damasio reassured me that science endorses Spinoza's argument that the mind knows itself by perceiving the ideas of the body's emotions, that "the mind is the idea of the body." (II.13) He theorizes that our feelings express "human flourishing or human distress, as they occur in mind and body." (Emotions are bodily, feelings are mental.)

I found it good to know that George Eliot, Spinoza's first English translator, found calm of mind through translating his *Ethics Geometrically Demonstrated.*

In an epigraph in *Daniel Deronda* (II.16), she writes, "Men, like planets, have both a visible and an invisible history, ...hidden pathways of feeling and thought which lead up to every moment of action and to those moments of intense suffering which take the quality of action."

A narrator, she says, threads those hidden pathways. The journey is difficult and long, unique to each person, unique to each time and place.

It appealed to me that Spinoza's and Eliot's connections between the mind, emotions, and the body correspond well to the psychology of Vipassana and its wish for beings to be happy. "A person knows himself only by the affections of his own body and his idea of them. Therefore when it happens that the mind is able to think about itself, we suppose that by this very fact it is passing to a greater perfection, i.e. it is affected by joy, and the more distinctly it can imagine itself and its own power of action, the greater its joy." (III.53.Proof)

Spinoza's view of "adequate ideas" is like Buddha's "seeing things as they are."

He also appreciates precepts: "The best thing we can achieve, so long as we do not have perfect cognition of our emotions, is to conceive a right manner of living or sure tenets of life and to commit them to memory and apply them constantly to particular situations that often meet us in life, so that they may have a broad effect on our imagination and always be at hand for us." (V.10.Scholium)

By the end of the book I was convinced he was blessed, joyous, and wise.

I began to realize that many of the things I liked about him—the things most similar to Buddhism—had roots in Stoic philosophy. Therefore, for the second semester of my retirement, I assigned myself Marcus Aurelius's *Meditations* aka *To Himself*.

3.

I began my Marcus journey with the help of Pierre Hadot (1922-2010), a scholar known for his argument that ancient philosophy involves a way of life, a technique of inner living and communal art of living.

Hadot focuses on philosophical practice as a therapeutic spiritual exercise best pursued in dialogue with oneself and/or with others, not a theoretical, abstract academic activity.

The practice includes "speaking well, thinking well, acting well, being truly conscious of one's place in the cosmos."

Much like the engaged Buddhism that has come to shape my philosophy, it is to be applied in daily life.

The emphasis is on method and path rather than solution and goal. "It is possible," Hadot writes in *Philosophy as a Way of Life* (1995), "for modern man to live...as a practitioner of the ever-fragile *exercise* of wisdom."

I had read, liked, and taught Hadot's earlier book *Plotinus or the Simplicity of Vision* (1993).

I discovered that, as Hadot grew older, his passion shifted from mysticism to ethics, just as mine had. This led to his "way of life" view and his more recent book, *The Inner Citadel: The Meditations of Marcus Aurelius* (2001).

Hadot examines Marcus's meditations as spiritual exercises combining two Stoic therapeutic techniques. The first is the remembering of the words and rules of his Stoic teacher Epictetus. The second is the repetition of these rules as he writes them for himself so that they become active principles of his inner discourse, a more long-term process.

Hadot's argument is that "the Stoic philosophical life consists essentially in mastering one's inner discourse." That requires having precepts on hand.

In contrast, Buddhist *bhavana,* mental cultivation, and *lojong,* mind training, include the study of verbal dharma teachings, reflection on them, and meditation practice that lets go of words, concepts, precepts, and inner discourse, a more long-term process.

Marcus writes in Greek, Epictetus's philosophical language, to internalize the terms, precepts, and teachings correctly. I got the Greek text to follow along.

In the first chapter, he reflects on all those in his life who had provided him with good models and good instruction.

Among these, his friend Rusticus made him aware that he "needed amendment and training (*therapeia*)," and gave him, from his own library, a book of notes taken in Epictetus's classes (*hypomnemata,* "notes intended to help one remember"). (I.7)

I began taking notes as I read to help me remember.

In keeping with Stoic therapeutic practice, Marcus is addressing himself. He is not writing advice for some other "you." He notes, between Books I and II, that he writes "among the Quadi on the Gran," camped on the Danube frontier. (The Germanic barbarians he was fighting were probably my ancestors.)

People seek solitary retreats in remote places, he notes, and he is tempted to do so. He reminds himself, "Nowhere can a man find a retreat more full of peace or free from care than his own soul.... Make use of this retirement continually and regenerate yourself....Let your axioms be short and elemental, such as when set before you will at once rid you of all trouble." (IV.3)

He tells himself, "We have come into being for co-operation, as have the feet, the hands, the eyelids, the rows of upper and lower teeth. Therefore to thwart one another is against nature, and we do thwart one another by showing resentment and aversion." (II.1)

He reminds himself of the transience of the vital breath and the body, and that he should not let his *hegemonikon* (guiding principle, rational soul) be jerked about by them like a puppet or have resentment or aversion toward what the nature of things brings about. Only his rational mind, in the present moment, is in his power. (II.2)

"See things in all their naked reality." (IV.11)

He constantly trains himself to remember impermanence and the brevity of life. "Unceasingly contemplate the generation of all things through change. Accustom yourself to the thought that the nature of the universe delights above all in changing the things that exist and making new uses of the same pattern." (IV.36)

He considers other ways of seeing things but finds the holistic view and his ethics are inseparable. "Either there is a well-arranged order of things, or a maze, indeed, but not without a plan. Or can a sort of order subsist in you, while in the universe there is no order, and that too when all things, though separated and dispersed, are still in sympathetic connection?" (IV.27)

His holistic sense of the universe sometimes borders on the mystical. "Cease not to think of the universe as one living being, possessed of a single substance and a single soul, and how all things trace back to its single sentience, and how it does all things by a single impulse, and how all existing things are joint causes of all things that come into existence, and how intertwined in the fabric is the thread and how closely woven the web." (IV.40)

For me, his most memorable thoughts follow from this inseparability:

"Consider each tiny plant, each little bird, the ant, the spider, the bee, how they go about their own work and each do his part for the building up of an orderly universe." (V.1)

"That which is not in the interests of the hive cannot be in the interests of the bee." (VI.54)

"We come into the world for the sake of one another." (XI.18)

4.

When I finished the *Meditations* book, I wanted to socialize my inner discourse with "sympathetic connection" and seek out therapeutic dialogue with others.

I started attending some reading-based discussion groups in my community.

One group was working its way, week by week, chapter by chapter, through *Devotions for People Who Don't Do Devotions,* a 2023 book by Tim Schenck, an Episcopal priest, offering "small morsels of real life to be chewed upon."

While reading Marcus, I kept thinking how there's an intimate devotional tone in his relationship to his teachers, his guiding soul, human society, and the universe, without either Epictetus's doctrinal rigor or the Biblical weight of a personal Creator or divine judgment.

Hadot talks about how Christianity took over, in a more popular way, ancient philosophy's role in offering a way of life. In this tradition, the *Devotions* book is set up as a personal and communal spiritual exercise for people with busy lives.

Each topic has a key phrase, a short Biblical quote, a homily drawn from everyday secular life, and a "Reflect and Engage" section offering two or three questions for personal reflection and group discussion.

The women in the group are, like me, of grandparental age, politically liberal, several of us recently retired teachers, missing our purpose which depended on others.

We have no one to teach but ourselves.

Our topic for this week is "Staying Focused." The quote is from Habakkuk: "Write the vision; make it plain on tablets, so that a runner may read it."

Meanwhile the tag on my Yogi tea bag reads, "Smiling is the most basic kind of peacework."

The Prayer Chain

When she cannot sleep,
she takes down from where it hangs by her bed
a rosary that belonged to her aunt whom she loved,
whom she wished were her mother.

She has it here now, in her pocket.
Out comes a rosary with stones blue as her eyes
going blind under thick glasses,
cross and chain silver gray like her hair.
She remembers from childhood (she is 91)
the sequence of Creed, Our Father, Hail Mary, Glory Be,
as do other former Catholics in the room, unlike me.

When she cannot sleep,
she prays for each person in the church, circling through
where each sits on Sunday at morning prayer
as if each were a bead. Then she prays,
as if counting beads on the chain with the cross,
for those for whom people have requested
prayers from the prayer chain.

I receive her calls,
her voice halting, fragile, precise, telling me
the first name and concern of each person.
Using mala and tonglen for rosary and creed,
I breathe in the concerns and breathe out a blessing on those names,
also a blessing on Betty, who is learning to see without eyes.

Art and Death

1.

My last two years before retiring were the first two years college classes opened after the closings from the covid pandemic. I began teaching a new in-person humanities course, Art and Death, which someone had proposed and gotten approved but it had never been taught. Against expectation, the class filled immediately.

The majority of students on campus were first generation college students. Many of them and many of their family members were essential workers during covid. Some family members were among those who had died. Some of their grandparents died in hospitals or in far-off countries without their being able to visit them.

The classes broke up into discussions where students shared their stories and concerns about death, a subject we typically avoid speaking about even when it is the elephant in the room. A disturbing thing that came up was their awareness of suicide postings on social media, including filmed suicides and advice on how to do it. The students agreed that they couldn't resist returning to posts that upset them.

Their fast-changing social media world, exacerbated by covid isolation, was a completely different world from the traditional humanities world I inhabited. This was not yet the case in the sixties during the early years of my teaching experience. Gradually, over the next fifty years, humanities and their focus on books and close readings fell out of educational fashion. This change included a disinterest in western philosophical, spiritual, and religious texts, though not in more sociological phenomena like occultism or witchcraft, or in non-western traditions.

In the Art and Death course I tried to alternate between assigned readings in books and on-line visual arts, music, and theatrical performances. Students couldn't be counted upon to buy or borrow a book or e-book, much less to read it. Because of the existential nature of our topic, I just let this be. For example,

I assigned Sophocles's *Oedipus at Colonus* but what we watched and talked about was the performance of *The Gospel at Colonus,* an African-American gospel music adaptation, with Morgan Freeman as a Pentecostal preacher and the Blind Boys of Alabama as Oedipus.

One of the most moving things that emerged was the students' tender memories of their departed grandparents, who seemed to represent to them a lost art of living, a fragile legacy.

I stopped teaching because the college, in a budget crisis, cut back on humanities funding and I lost my contract. I was in my early eighties. Although I felt and still feel vigorous, there was no question but that I was getting old and that dying and death lay in my foreseeable future. How was I to prepare for that? What practical experience might previous thoughtful and sympathetic humans have to give me? How might I teach Art and Death to myself, without the need to consider what would be meaningful to students sixty years younger than I was?

I took an approach to this project similar to my smaller project of playing Goldberg Variations on the piano. I allow myself to exclude those variations written for two keyboards that I can't easily play on one keyboard unless I were to acquire more fingers. My rule is complexity within the limits of ease.

2.

During the second semester of my first year after retiring, after my first semester focus on Spinoza, I educated myself with readings from Stoic, Epicurean, and Cynic philosophical traditions, all of which, committed to pursuing happiness, *eudaimonia,* believe it is attained through equanimity, *ataraxia*, the art and practice of accepting things, including death, that you can't do anything about. Philosophy for them is an art of living.

I went on to read Montaigne as an heir to these traditions, one who is relaxed about mixing them together. "I believe in and conceive a thousand contrary ways of life" (I.37) seems to me a worthy credo. His writing slithers out of structure and system.

In Sarah Bakewell's *How to Live or a Life of Montaigne in One Question and Twenty Attempts at an Answer* (2010), two of the attempted answers are "live temperately" and "pay attention," which fit in with my Buddhist practice and octogenarian inclinations.

In "Of Moderation," Montaigne writes that he likes "temperate and moderate natures." He thinks philosophy should be practical, not excessive or extreme. "In its excess," he says, "it enslaves our natural freedom and, by importunate subtlety, leads us astray from the fine and level road that nature has traced for us." (I.30)

Yes, as my knees know, I need a fine and level road, no steep uphill or down, no stones to stumble over. My mind too needs clarity and illumination, not knots and snarls.

Montaigne often brings up Socrates as his model of the wisest man. Socrates's wisdom was that he knew that he knew nothing. He never flaunted pretentious knowledge or exalted himself.

Yes, I find that I can't remember what I once thought I knew or flaunted. It has evaporated like a dream. I no longer know much of anything.

What Socrates did know, says Montaigne, was how to "lead the life of man in conformity with its natural condition." Alexander merely knew how to subdue the world, whereas for Montaigne "the value of the soul consists not in flying high, but in an orderly pace. Its greatness is exercised not in greatness, but in mediocrity." (III.2)

Yes, I've given up on mountain climbing and lofty ambitions. My vision is more limited and falling is risky. In all spheres of life an orderly pace relaxes the mind and the body.

"What unseats [the soul], what casts it most commonly into insanity," Montaigne argues, "but its quickness, its keenness, its agility, and in short its very strength? Of what is the subtlest madness made, but the subtlest wisdom?" Slow down!

This touches a bitter truth, as I witness old friends' mental decline and mental illness in young people who are dear to my heart. Montaigne's view of what unseats us is in response to the particular insanity of the poet Tasso, whom he visited in a madhouse in Ferrara. (Montaigne prefers the equanimous Epicurean poets Horace and Lucretius.)

Nietzsche, whom I regard as an icon of quickness and immoderation leading to insanity, was a great fan of Montaigne, whom he called "this freest and mightiest of souls." Hölderlin, a poet with the subtlest wisdom, retired to a tower for forty years after losing his mind. When I was younger, I was drawn to their extremes.

Sarah Bakewell describes the round tower of Montaigne's ancestral chateau to which, in 1571, when he was thirty-eight and having a midlife crisis, he retired from public service to live "in calm and freedom from all cares" in "the bosom of the learned Virgins [the Muses]."

Originally designed for defense, the tower had an overview of the surrounding countryside and the rest of the chateau, including his wife's tower on the opposite side.

Montaigne ascended the floors of his tower by a spiral staircase, winding from the chapel on the ground floor up to his bedroom and then to his library on the third floor, below the attic where a loud bell tolled the hours. Around a thousand books occupied five rows of curving shelves fitted to the round tower. Also displayed were his collections of family heirlooms, historical artefacts, and assorted curiosities. He had the roofbeams painted with classical quotations such as Pliny the Elder's "only one thing is certain, that nothing is certain" and Terence's "I am human, I consider nothing human foreign to me."

It is in this round space, engaged with the round space of his mind, that he contemplated, read, and wrote.

Bakewell observes how, in the twenty-year course of writing his essays, he "seems to have achieved an almost Zen-like discipline, an ability to just *be.*" Writing essays became his way of paying attention to himself, of observing his mind, its abundant variety.

In his 1573-74 essay "Of Practice" (II.6), namely the practice of portraying his "cogitations," he observes, "It is a thorny undertaking, and more so than it seems, to follow a movement so wandering as that of our mind, to penetrate the opaque depths of its innermost folds, to pick out and immobilize the innumerable flutterings that agitate it."

Earlier in "Of Practice" he pointed out that, while death is "the greatest task we have to perform, practice cannot help us" since we only get one try at it. He goes on to examine his experience of a near-fatal riding accident, what the incident taught him, how it got him "used to the idea of death." Being "used to the idea of death," he engages wholeheartedly with life and considers himself to be without melancholy temperament.

The students in the Art and Death course were assigned to develop essays and give presentations interacting with the assigned and/or their choice of art works, their in-class discussions, and their thoughts and personal experiences. Even the most hesitant ones began to speak and write of getting used to the idea of death and talking about it, something they had not imagined would be possible.

3.

When the Norwegian author Jon Fosse won the 2023 Nobel Prize in literature, an article described him as a writer who practices solitude, a convert to Roman Catholicism for whom writing is a confession, a prayer, a way of asking for forgiveness. His writing is said to be influenced by Ibsen and Beckett on the one hand, the Bible and Meister Eckhart on the other. *Melancholy I* and *Melancholy II* are among his previous novels. *Septology,* his 2019 seven-novel trilogy, is his most ambitious, spiritual, and innovative work.

In Merve Emre's 2022 *New Yorker* interview with Fosse, Emre wrote, "*Septology* is the only novel I have read that has made me believe in the reality of the divine." I was intrigued, since the mystical, the divine, the sacred are my province of study. These rarely appear in contemporary literature, and I often feel alone in wanting to read, write, and talk about them.

Emre reports that the Norwegian Foreign Minister quoted Wittgenstein at a Fosse Foundation dinner: "Whereof one cannot speak, thereof one must be silent." In the interview, Fosse comments on Derrida's revision: "'What you cannot say, you have to write.' That's closer to the way I think about it." Fosse tells how he had been a student of philosophy. Both Derrida and Heidegger contributed to his "thought that the act of writing is something very peculiar," very different from speaking.

There is a lot of repetition in Fosse's writing, which is in a rural Norwegian dialect, Nynorsk. He develops the inner monologue stream of Asle, the narrator of *Septology,* as if it were his slow subliminal process of learning to die. It continuously interweaves recollections of his life story with the present action of the novel, which includes the alcoholic death of his alter ego, and takes place, beginning on a Monday, in the week before Christmas, ending on Christmas Eve.

Septology's first six books begin, with slight verbal variations, "And I see myself standing and looking at the picture with the two lines that cross in the middle..." The seventh and last book begins, "And I see myself standing there looking at the painting in the pile with the stretcher facing out..." Asle has come to feel it is time to give up his lifelong vocation as a painter.

Each book ends with Asle praying as he holds the rosary with a brown wooden cross given him by his late beloved wife Ales and tries to fall asleep. The first chapter ends with the Hail Mary final words, *et in hora mortis nostrae,* "and in the hour of our death." The prayer "Christ have mercy on me" ends chapters two through six. The last chapter ends with the Hail Mary uncompleted, *et in hora.* By implication, silence follows, death follows. The trilogy is threaded through with a number of such subtly shifting repetitions. They build up to a climax with the end of the narrator's verbalized mind stream.

In Emre's interview, he asks Fosse whether he often thinks about death. Fosse replies, "No. I think the closer you get, the older you get, the less you think about it. I think it was Cicero who said that philosophy is a way of learning to die. And I think literature is also a way of learning to die. It's as much about death as about life." He adds, "Art is alive when you create it, and there's a reader who can bring it to life again. But as an object it's dead."

Fosse, who was born in 1959, began writing the trilogy in 2012 after he became Catholic and quit drinking. It is his longest work (667 pages in the English translation), involving a practice called "slow prose." Although we read quite a few theological essays surfacing through Asle's mind stream, Fosse says that he edited out more than a hundred of them on the advice of his editor. In the novel, Ales, Asle's wife, an icon painter, initiates his conversion, rosary and prayer practice, and interest in theology.

In *Wittgenstein's Ladder: Poetic Language and the Strangeness of the Ordinary* (1996), Marjorie Perloff writes about Wittgenstein's unintentional minimalist impact on the language of poets and writers. Her 2022 edition of Wittgenstein's *Private Notebooks 1914-1916* reveals details about his early spiritual preoccupations and his efforts to express them within his strict linguistic constraints.

Wittgenstein kept the notebooks while he was a soldier during the Great War. He wrote of his emotions and spiritual struggles in coded language on the left side of the notebooks. Logic, philosophical ambition, intellectual struggle and notes for a draft of the *Tractatus* are on the right. In the final form of the *Tractatus*, the concluding paragraphs append death and the problem of life, the concerns of the coded left, to the exhaustive logical argument of the predominant text. Mystical and metaphysical solutions to the riddle of life, they argue, "cannot be put into words. They make themselves manifest." (6.522) They are what, as he says in the Preface, "lies on the other side of the limits of language."

Wittgenstein's logical structure, "the scaffolding of the world" (6.124), is articulated in six parts, and on the seventh there's a sabbath of silence. The Book of Revelation too is structured around sevens followed by a vision of a new heaven and a new earth. *Septology* opens with an epigraph from Revelation: "And I will give him a white stone, and on the stone a new name written, which no one knows except him who receives it." The title of the last part of the trilogy is "A New Name" (VI-VII).

In one of Asle's inner monologues, while he is contemplating the picture with the two lines that cross in the middle, he tells how he shuts the curtain to see it in the dark, because "the shining darkness that I'm always trying to paint is visible in the darkness." He enters one of his theological reflections and thinks about how little he understands, how living bodies die yet "the invisible human being is still there...yes, the invisible eye is still there after the visible one is gone, because what's inside the eye, inside the person, doesn't go away, because there's God inside the person, it's the kingdom of God there, yes, as stands written [in the Gospel]."

Both Fosse and Asle are readers of the mystic Meister Eckhart, who wrote, "The soul has two eyes: an inner and an outer eye." "The eye with which I see God is the same as the eye with which God sees me."

Elsewhere Asle reflects on how the pictures in his head have sorrow and pain and also a kind of peace. His goal is to paint them away so that only the peace stays behind. In the interview, Fosse says, "It's the wholeness that's the soul of writing. The message comes from the wholeness of its silent language."

4.

As in Bach's keyboard music where several voices are interplayed by two hands and ten fingers, my mental fingers explore how themes weave apart and together. The speed is andante moderato. The volume is low. Variations manifest, like the voices of insects and birds at dawn and dusk, from spring to the sleep of winter and a new spring.

It is nearing summer's end now, the end of my first year and beginning of my second year of retirement. In the evening, the quietude of plants, as they rest from growth and bask in the lowering sun, underlies the chorus of cicadas. For the rise of the equinoctial full moon, the local Japanese stroll garden will gather us around a frog pond to listen, over the drone of stillness, to frog songs and the Zen tones of bamboo flute and koto, repetitive, sparse, lento.

I enjoyed Fosse's/Asle's dronelike, repetitive yet pressing inner voice. From my Buddhist rather than Catholic perspective, Asle's mantric continuum of prayer and recollection suggests a meditative relaxation of mind allowing for calm awareness and letting go of the turnings of sentient life, the realm of samsara.

This has been the first year when several friends in my age group have died after lengthy debilitation. Previous deaths close to me were premature or of elders when they were old. My younger self's vague poetic inner sense of melancholy has strangely faded like the hum of my previous tinnitus, has been lifted away like the dark scrim of my cataracts, though my taste for a few melancholic voices, alive or in writing, lingers.

Bond

I was moved when she said
she found strange comfort
by lying on her mother's grave
though her mother was not a good person.

Prostrate, heart to heart,
breast to breast, womb to womb,
she weeps libations
at the door of the dead.

It seems to mean (though I do not know)
that a force of pain rests in that place.
She may have seen how, in death,
her mother's face was quiet.

In my bad dreams, she said,
I become aware, it's a dream.
I know that, to awaken,
I must die in the dream.

Her eyes are bright as she speaks.
She seems calm and steady,
poised to stay awake,
to speak of her mother.

Aging with Lucretius, Venus, and Buddha

1.

Lately I have been taking delight in the poetry of Lucretius, who took delight in Epicurus's philosophy, which he called *vera ratio,* a true account, bringing clarity and calm into thought.

Reading Lucretius is like seeing a bunch of white lambs playing on green grass in the springtime when colors are just coming forth from their winter's sleep, or like falling in love with life.

A fellow invoker and devotee of goddesses, Lucretius takes as his muse Venus, nurturing mother, goddess of beauty and love, source of pleasures, ruler of the nature of things, "through whom every living thing is conceived and rises up to behold the light of the sun."

On her lap, Mars god of war settles down and "things joyous and lovely come forth into the shining borders of light." Mars, inner and outer, settle down!

Birth as coming forth into light reminds me of Iphigenia's plea at Aulis, "No longer the light, / no longer the rays of the sun / belong to me," and of Antigone's epode, "No longer am I allowed to see this holy light of the sun," as each woman stands without justice at the edge of the dark below.

Lucretius is not bothered about death as the other side of light's borders. Epicurus taught him to think of the boundaries of life's pleasures and pains, how "removal of all that causes pain marks the boundary of pleasures," how death is in the compostable nature of things coming together and falling apart, how reason tells us death is not to be feared though our troublesome religious superstitions might habituate us to think otherwise. They might even, as Lucretius points out, cause a sinless person such as Iphigenia to be the victim of a sinful crime.

As an aging Buddhist and a follower of the sciences of well-being, I am in accord with Epicurus's acceptance of impermanence, disease, aging, and death as part of the nature of things, and his turning to reason and natural science to help us address "our inability to discern the limits of our vexatious pains and desires" so that we cause ourselves and others more pain and harm.

In Buddha's diagnosis, our suffering is caused by our ignorance about the nature of things, so that we want things to be otherwise than they are. He offers a path of thought, action, and meditation that leads to happiness. It is a middle way between austerity and extravagance.

Epicurus adds to his path a hedonism of modest limits which I find particularly suitable for these octogenarian years when in any case pleasures have limits and, for example, I avoid doing things that offend my joints, digestion, or sleep, and hope to avoid the pain of outlasting my vital span.

Epicurean hedonism relayed by Lucretius embellishes my Buddhist practice with sensuality and poetry. Instead of ascetic meditation in a nunnery or a Himalayan cave, meditation by a stream in a garden like the garden in Andrew Marvell's poem (wherein the mind "withdraws into its happiness" and everything becomes "a green thought in a green shade") weaves together Epicurus's Garden, Buddha's sacred world, and a poem close to my heart, as it was the focus of my late husband's dissertation, now more than a half century ago, when we were students and Venus and poetry drew us together.

Lucretius's inspiration for mixing reasoning and science with poetic hexameters was Empedocles's *On Nature*, which tells of how things, comprised of four elements (air, fire, earth, and water), come together through *Philia,* Love, and fall apart through *Neikos,* Strife.

Nothing is created or destroyed, only mixed and exchanged in stages rarifying and condensing, combining and separating, without beginning or ending.

"Look on Love with your mind," he advises us, "not with your eyes. She is known inborn in mortal limbs. With her think lovingly and do peaceful deeds."

Among the ancient Greek philosophers, Empedocles was the last to put his philosophy into verse. Only fragments survive in the writings of others who quote bits much the way I'm quoting bits now.

2.

In his late twenties at the end of the 18th century, when the vicissitudes of Love and Strife dominated his politics and his life, my favorite German poet, Friedrich Hölderlin, composed what has been called a masterpiece in fragments, three uncompleted versions of a tragedy or, as he called it, a *trauerspiel*, a mourning-play, *The Death of Empedocles.*

Hölderlin was from Swabian Württemberg, the southwest German state from which the families of my maternal grandparents came to America.

On the political side, he was among those inspired by the French revolution with hopes to reform autocratic rule in his state and create a democratic republic.

Serving as a tutor, he fell in love with Susette Gontard, the mother of his pupil, and made her his muse, calling her Diotima after Socrates's teacher in the art of love as told in the *Symposium.*

Hölderlin wrote of her to his friend Christian-Neuffer, "My sense of beauty is now secure from all disruption... My intellect attends her school and my riven inmost heart daily finds repose and good cheer in her all-sufficient peace."

A few months later, after gossip about the affair got out and the husband was in the know, Hölderlin wrote to his friend, "I am torn asunder by love and hate."

In a short ode "To Diotima" he wrote: "...your beauty lives like tender flowers in winter, / in the altered world you bloom hidden, alone... / your sun has gone under, / storms moan in frosty night."

Jobless, separated from his Diotima, he began writing the first version of *The Death of Empedocles,* reading Diogenes Laertius's *Lives of the Eminent Philosophers* Book VIII on Empedocles's life and opinions, and closely identifying with Empedocles.

The most well-known story about Empedocles is that he died by throwing himself into the flames of Mt. Etna.

Along with being a poet, scientist, philosopher, healer, mystic, and orator, he was a democratic activist when antidemocratic greed and unwisdom were taking over Agrigentum, his city.

Hölderlin's contemporary, the poet Novalis, wrote, "The genuine philosophical act is suicide; this is the real beginning of all philosophy."

As Hölderlin was reading and thinking about Empedocles and working on his mourning-play, he wrote in a letter, "the transiency and mutability of human thoughts and systems strike me as well-nigh more tragic than the destinies one usually calls the only real destinies."

He asks, "where then does the human being rule supreme...if he depends on foreign influences in autonomous thought itself?" He adds that it's a good thing that "no force rules monarchically."

In his essay on "The Ground for Empedocles," he concludes, "It is the most profound inwardness that expresses itself in the tragic dramatic poem... nothing whatever can be understood and animated, if we cannot translate our own mood and our own experience in a foreign analogic matter."

Hölderlin wrote four essays developing his theory of the tragic. Running through his thinking is a basic opposition, repeatedly intensifying into conflict, between art and nature, between the poet's or self-conscious individual's world and soul and mode of being, and his need to make this feeling knowable, to "depict itself by separating itself off from itself in the excess of intensity in which opposites mistake themselves for one another," thus surrendering itself too much to nature and forgetting itself.

Describing a complex interplay of subjective and objective extremes mixing and mistaking and reversing themselves, he sees Empedocles as someone in whom "the supreme opposition between nature and art, and the real excess of intensity...come to the fore on the basis of enmity and supreme conflict. ...In him art and nature unite in extreme antagonism, the active in excess becomes objective, and the subjectivity that has been lost is replaced by the profound encroachment of the object."

In contrast, "when life is pure, nature and art oppose one another merely harmoniously. Art is the blossom, the perfection of nature."

In the third version, Hölderlin interprets and identifies himself with Empedocles's tragedy as hubristic overreach in his attempted fusion with nature. That must be purged and purified.

After writing the four essays and three play versions and before losing his mind, he worked on translations of Pindar's odes and wrote the poems for which he is most known, where his art fully blossoms and comes into its own, where he is able to transpose his own inmost heart and experience to the foreign analogical material of Swabian nature, ancient Greece, and prophecy.

Michael Hamburger, the great translator of Hölderlin, writes of how, in his works and in his life, his "progression was one through contraries, through conflicts strenuously fought out, and leaps into the unknown."

Conflict is gone from his late poems written after his plunge into schizophrenia.

Although Hölderlin was far from being a Lucretian Epicurean hedonist, Hamburger points out how he had a committed pantheist's absolute and religious faith in the powers and processes of nature, such that "he could dissolve works of his own, just as organic nature dissolves its phenomena, so that new growth can develop from the dissolution....no less than his works, to him the producers of poems, too, were only vessels that could be broken when they had served their purpose. Goethe wanted to preserve his person, and therefore left his contraries to run along parallel lines, sometimes making a game of them. Hölderlin had to enact his to the point of self-destruction."

Hamburger adds: "There is no need to point to the present relevance of a dead earth....More consistently than Goethe's, Hölderlin's 'natural piety' insisted on bounds set to the human urge to know and to exploit knowledge."

3.

Reading Hölderlin and Empedocles, like reading Homer and the Greek tragedians, resonates with my sense of conflict in the nature of things, including in my mind prone to self-conflict and easily agitated by external conflict.

Yoga, Buddhism, and the Platonic, Stoic, and Epicurean traditions, ancient philosophies and arts of living, help me cultivate harmony and peace of mind and a sense of friendly community, which I increasingly value as I age.

It took me all these years, from my first reading more than sixty years ago, to appreciate Lucretius's transformation of epic from a dramatic narrative of heroic destruction to a peaceable narrative of nature's generous order. During these years, we humans have increasingly exploited that generosity and increased our capacity for destroying ourselves and our world.

In Lucretius's philosophy, things continually come together, fall apart, come together again. "No visible object utterly passes away, since nature makes up again one thing from another, and does not permit anything to be born unless aided by another's death." (I.262-264)

Nature's birth-giving beauty in springtime energizes the beauty of his poetry and the beauty of his way of life.

Among pre-Socratic philosophers, he most attacks Heraclitus, who taught that "strife is right," that "war is the father, and king of all," and that fire is the primary substance. Since fire is all-consuming, Lucretius argues, it follows that it consumes itself and then creates itself from nothing, which defies reason and sense. He praises Empedocles for "the poems of his divine mind" (I.731) and Empedocles's homeland Sicily, "famed as a place to see, fat with good things" (I.727-728) because of Etna's spectacular raging forces that stimulate fecundity. "There is in famed Etna nothing more illustrious than this man, nor more sacred and wonderful and dear." (I.729).

The Vajrayana Buddhism I practice similarly sees violent natural forces as energies to be tamed by clarifying our relationship to them. Potentially destructive psychological forces (fear, anger, lust, hate) can be transformed into creative awareness of the way things are.

At present, I and my agemates confront our decline and death at a time when modern comforts and medical science have enabled more than three times as many of us to live over sixty than lived over sixty around the time when we were born. A quarter of people in the United States are now over sixty. More than 147 million people, almost two percent of the world's more than eight billion population, are in my cohort, 80-99 years old. There are almost a hundred million more of us over sixty-five than those under five. Caring for us has become a lucrative industry, while funding and support for education and training of our descendants is in crisis.

Along with reading Lucretius, I am reading a book by Samuel Harrington, MD, *At Peace: Choosing a Good Death After a Long Life* (2018), arguing against people past normal life expectancy choosing overly aggressive institutionalized medical interventions in the natural processes of declining and dying.

Lucretius argues against fears from superstitious beliefs about gods causing suffering in this life and in an imagined afterlife. Harrington argues against excessive faith in what the medical-industrial complex has to offer us. The problem, he says, is our fear and denial of death.

We become sick, says Lucretius, because "multitudinous seeds of things exist, and our earth and sky contain enough harmful germs to allow measureless amounts of diseases to be produced." (VI.662-664) It is, in any case, in the nature of things that "all things gradually decay and head for the reef of destruction, exhausted by long lapse of time." (II.1173-1174)

Similarly, he sings, among the multitudinous seeds of things, there are primary elements that, variously ordered in words and lines, bring about his poem. (I.822-829)

In Epicurus's as well as Buddha's philosophical approach to life and death, the cultivation of equanimity increases our happiness and decreases our suffering. Equanimity also provides a middle way between the polarities Buddha calls the eight worldly dharmas of our desires and aversions: pleasure/pain, gain/loss, praise/blame, fame/disrepute.

Flavoring Epicurus's sober prose reasoning with "the Muses's delicious honey," Lucretius writes to persuade his unsober poetic friend Memmius of Epicurus's wisdom, as well as out of his own love of the Muses and his hope for glory.

"O pitiable minds of mortals," he sings, "...to think that you should fail to see that nature importunately demands only that the body may be rid of pain, and that the mind, divorced from impiety and fear, may enjoy a feeling of contentment." (II.15-19)

4.

Buddha's teaching about suffering and happiness is summarized in the *Dhammapada's* opening verses. "Mind is the forerunner of all actions." From speech or action done with an impure mind, suffering follows "as the wheel follows the hoof of an ox pulling a cart." Happiness follows, "as surely as one's shadow," if one speaks or acts with a pure mind. "He abused me, he beat me, he defeated me, he robbed me –hatred never ceases in one harboring those thoughts.... Hatred ceases by love. This is a timeless truth (*sanatana dharma*)." Venus settles Mars down.

Therigata: Poems of the First Buddhist Women is the first known anthology of women's literature. One of the women, Ambapali, was a courtesan and poet famous for her beauty about whom I once wrote a spicy novel that never got published. She was a lay follower of Buddha until her old age, when she "went forth" and sang, in twenty verses, of the places, head to toe, where her beauty had disappeared. Each verse is followed by the refrain, "it's just as the Buddha, the speaker of truth, said, / nothing different than that." She begins with the truth that "the hairs on my head were once curly, / black, like the color of bees, / now because of old age / they are like jute." The last verse sums up: "this body was once like that, / now feeble with age and fallen from its pride, / it is the home of many sufferings, / like an old house, the plaster falling down."

These women of early Buddhism sing of being at peace, no longer encumbered by the urges of Venus aka Kama, erotic desire and the fecund upsurges of springtime. I have never felt inclined to be thus disencumbered.

Fortunately, as Buddhism developed, celibacy became but one of many paths to enlightenment. Milarepa (1051-1135), an unmarried but not celibate yogi, sings of the power of his guru and dharma, as well as of the beauty of the Himalayan mountains and valleys and women he meets there. He sings as he wanders into his eighty-fourth year, an almost naked Shiva-like yogi in a loose cotton cloth, his "male jewel" hanging out. He is famous for having become enlightened in one lifetime.

There are, it is said, 84,000 doors to enlightenment, and innumerable variations suited to the karmic condition of each person. Milarepa killed people out of revenge when he was young. The Great Vehicle message is that the karmic energies of both Venus and Mars can be transformed from suffering into enlightenment.

Lama Yeshe's *Introduction to Tantra: The Transformation of Desire* (1987) presents advanced practices for skillfully using these energies. "It is only through the skillful use of desirous energy and by building up the habit of experiencing what we might call true pleasure that we can hope to achieve the everlasting bliss and joy of full illumination... Grasping and attachment is the problem, not the pleasures themselves."

Lucretius describes in some detail our unskillful desirous passions, "that honeyed drop of Venus's sweetness that first trickles into our heart, to be followed by frigid care." (IV.1059-1060) He reasons, "it is undeniable that the pleasure of intercourse is purer for the healthy-minded than for the lovesick." (IV.1075-1976)

Meditation, age's gradual process of letting go, and the wake-up shocks of loss have opened me to what feels like a more pure and skillful use of desirous energy, with more ability to join in touch without grasping, to be thankful for friendship and whatever togetherness remains possible. A recent AARP magazine article, "Dodge Your Biggest Health Risks," endorses making time for Venus as its fourth and final recommendation for dodging Risk #1, heart disease. "It's about the emotional connection," it says, "at a time when we are more likely to feel isolated."

5.

My next step, when at my body's death I cross beyond the boundary of the physical world imagined by Epicurus and Lucretius, falls outside the reasoning of their view. They reject belief in an afterlife as fear-based religious superstition.

On the other hand, the belief in reincarnation is very much part of Buddhism. To explore this view in the context of old age, I have begun rereading Sogyal Rinpoche's *The Tibetan Book of Living and Dying* (1992), which I first read shortly after it came out and shortly after my husband's sudden death, at 52, by a heart attack.

In my younger years, up until my husband's death when I was 50, I resonated with the teachings of Plato, the Upanishads, and the Bhagavad Gita, all of which assume reincarnation, the immortality of the soul, and a culminating experience of mystical union. At the same time, I practiced yoga meditation and studied Samkhya-Yoga philosophy, which has parallels with Buddhism, except that it observes the interactions between Nature and Consciousness (Prakriti and Purusha) and the practices by which our individual Purusha becomes able to distinguish its peaceful awareness from Nature's energetic vicissitudes.

There are subtle and interesting psychological differences among these schools of thought and how they articulate awareness and imagine reincarnation. Realization is beyond name, form, image, or concept, which are nevertheless needed to describe it and which carry the flavors of individual experiences and cultures. I like the Vedic saying, "truth is one, poets [and those experiencing it] speak of it in many ways." This allows a pragmatic approach, something for everyone and for one's evolving situation.

Where I am now, beginning to think about pragmatic preparations for advanced age, death, and the possibility of a beyond, the Great Vehicle bodhisattva prayer continues to be my most perfect guide: "As long as space endures, / As long as there are sentient beings to be found, / May I continue likewise to remain / To soothe the sufferings of those who live." The words, from Shantideva's eighth-century Sanskrit philosophical poem, *The Bodhisattva's Way of Life,* vow an intention and aspiration to perfect one's compassion and wisdom. The path is the goal. It is morally hedonistic, in that its guidance decreases suffering and generates happiness.

Snow

A solitary bird left behind
a delicate trail on new-fallen snow.

Perhaps he came briefly down from the air
to eat the bright crystals.

The flakes are light, fluffed up like foam,
each a study in pattern.

They stay fluffed white on my lashes and hair,
on the gray whiskers of a dog in a red coat.

Did the bird's tongue savor their melt
like we savor gelato?

My father used to gather snow in a bowl
and pour syrup in a ribbon that congealed into taffy.

After playing in the snow, we sat by the fire,
plucked the taffy and dozed off.

The snow's glare makes me sleepy.
My eyes squint and close. I drift like the snow drifts.

I give way to the cold and the all-white,
the quiet, the monotony, the pause.

Subtle Wanderings

1.

Now in my eighties, I have set up my "Advanced Directives." This allows me to concentrate on the spiritual side of aging and death while avoiding non-palliative medical interventions.

Perhaps because I have always liked learning and school, whether as a student or teacher, I tend to think of this life and its befores and afters as a process of education. Having spent my days wandering in the woods, fields, and gardens of poetry, philosophy, and religion while avoiding their deserts, I have harvested a variety of views about the soul, dying, and what lies beyond.

For some reason, I have never believed that birth was the beginning and death is the end.

In my early twenties, when I started writing poetry as a spiritual practice—that is to say, a way of thinking about subtle intuitions—W. B. Yeats was my principal teacher. I posted these lines from his poem "Sailing to Byzantium" on my writing desk: "Nor is there singing school but studying / Monuments of its own magnificence."

I liked the extravagant aspiration proclaimed in the poem's third stanza: "O sages standing in God's holy fire / As in the gold mosaic of a wall, / Come from the holy fire, perne in a gyre, / And be the singing masters of my soul.... gather me / Into the artifice of eternity." I liked the insinuation that the poem, the prayer, and eternity are artifices of the poetic imagination.

Yeats was one of the few modern poets I knew of who wrote about the soul, cultivated spiritual vision, studied the classic mystical philosophies of Plato and Plotinus as well as the Indian and occult philosophies I was studying in graduate school, and recorded poetically his sense of self-division between the holy visions and dreams of his mystical side and the struggles of his social and political side. In this he was much like Friedrich Hölderlin, whom I later took as my teacher.

In a 1924 article Yeats wrote, "We condemn the art of modern Europe. No man can create, as did Shakespeare, Homer, Sophocles, who does not believe, with all his blood and nerve, that man's soul is immortal, for the evidence lies plain to all men that where that belief has declined, men have turned from creation to photography." This is how I felt in the sixties when I came of age.

Although recent surveys show that 83% of American adults believe that people have a non-physical soul or spirit (81% believe in God, 73% believe in heaven, 62% in hell, 20% in reincarnation), philosophical or aesthetic reflection on the soul and immortality is not as conspicuous in our culture as are technologies for dying people to choose cryonic suspension, the uploading of their consciousness, or space burial. The senior centers mushrooming across the country market for material comfort and often for luxury rather than spiritual or psychological counsel.

Yeats (1865-1939) was in his sixties when he wrote "Sailing to Byzantium." He had health issues and felt old, "a paltry thing, / a tattered coat upon a stick." The poem is his quintessential expression of the tension between his spiritual vision, expressed in the crafted artifices of poetry, arts, and ideas, and the less refined realities of life. His biographer Richard Ellmann writes, "The man who emerges from his poetry is a modern man...he is torn by inner division.... Every poem is a battleground...."

Along with Yeats, my "singing school" in those days included the 17th-century English metaphysical poets, especially Andrew Marvell, a favorite of my husband and the focus of his dissertation. Unlike Yeats, Marvell writes within a culture of poets writing and people reading metaphysical poetry. His poem "On a Drop of Dew" reflects classic Platonic thought about the soul's descent, rebirth, and spiritual reunion.

> See how the orient dew,
> Shed from the bosom of the morn
>   Into the blowing roses,
> Yet careless of its mansion new,
> For the clear region where 'twas born
>   Round in itself incloses....

So the soul, that drop, that ray
Of the clear fountain of eternal day,
Could it within the human flower be seen,
  Remembering still its former height,
  Shuns the sweet leaves and blossoms green,
  And, recollecting its own light,
Does, in its pure and circling thoughts, express
The greater heaven in an heaven less....

I read this poem at my husband's memorial service. He had died suddenly of a heart attack. We had never seriously talked or perhaps even thought about our personal religious beliefs concerning death and the afterlife. We had grown up in the same Methodist church community and, I think, took for granted that the soul is immortal and that gospel hymns speak truth in lines such as these: "Rise, my soul, and stretch thy wings, thy better portion trace; / Rise from transitory things toward heaven, thy native place..."

My graduate studies focused on the Neo-Platonic mystical tradition as it descended from Plato through Plotinus. The Renaissance scholar Ficino, the first translator of Plotinus from Greek into Latin, was a specialty of my mentor Paul Oskar Kristeller. Alain de Lille, the 12th-century theologian and poet whose work I was translating, did not have access to Plotinus, but drew from Latin texts influenced by his school. This influence appears in a well-known line from the text I was translating: "God is a circle whose center is everywhere and whose circumference is nowhere." Lots of centers, lots of dewdrops!

Twenty years later, when my father was dying, he patiently listened while I took it upon myself to present him with Plato's philosophy of immortality, although I must have done it more to reassure myself. My father was an engineer, a builder, and a practical man who had gone to Methodist church his whole life, probably without thinking much about it. His pastor at the time was a former engineer who was able to give him meaningful counsel. When death was near, the spirit of my father's mother came to him at the foot of the hospital bed where he lay at home. She reassured him that love would not be lost at death.

Over the years after my father's death, I distanced myself from my engagement with Christianity and the Platonic tradition. Spiritually and academically, I became increasingly committed to the study and practice of Indian philosophies of yoga and meditation, first in the Vedic, then in the Buddhist traditions. Now I tend to interpret the Western through my experience in the Eastern traditions.

In Platonic meditative and aesthetic reflection, love and beauty form a spiritual continuum between mortality and immortality, between gross and subtle experience, sensory experience and pure ideas, a continuum of relationship that parallels the role of meditation in yoga. However the meditation practices used by Socrates and Plotinus did not form a living lineage passed on down to our present time as did the Vedic and Buddhist lineages. Nevertheless, Platonic and Vedic philosophies fall within the patterns of what Aldous Huxley, outside of academic scruple, termed "The Perennial Philosophy." So do the Indigenous spiritualities I am familiar with.

The Methodist hymns I grew up with often express a Christian poetic version of Platonic Perennial Philosophy. "Love divine, all loves excelling," by Charles Wesley, rearticulates Socrates's ladder of love from Plato's *Symposium*. "For the beauty of the earth" yokes natural beauty to its divine source. I still enjoy hymn singing as a spiritual practice in congregation, like kirtan sung in yoga groups or prayers chanted in Tibetan sanghas.

As in the image of God as a circle, Perennial Philosophy testifies to a single Reality or Truth apprehended through ethical and spiritual practices that allow one's soul to vividly experience its deathless participation in that larger Reality. When we are preoccupied, as we usually are, by the grosser manifestations of that Reality, we may not see their connection to the whole.

An underlying premise of these traditions' mystical language is that subtle spiritual experiences do not happen in words, so speaking of them requires metaphors and symbols, an oblique approach.

It is easy, for those of us so inclined, to get high on Perennial Philosophy in one form or another, to feel the wings on our souls, how they fly into and out of our bodies. Indigenous cultures testify to this primal natural sense of souls not bound by the body, their rebirth, and the recirculating endlessness of life.

Indigenous survival depended on awareness of subtle interconnected vital energies. Contemporary culture, of which I am a part, depends instead on ever more rapidly developed refinements of science, technology, and artificial intelligence. The subtle, appropriated and commodified, is reduced from qualitative, expansive, and poetic evocation of experience to quantitative and reductive information.

Anthony Lane reports on examples of this reduction in his May 27, 2024 *New Yorker* Onward and Upward with Technology piece, "Abridged Too Far: The world according to Blinklist." The most absurdly abridged book he discusses is Wittgenstein's notoriously difficult *Tractatus Logico-Philosophicus.* It is reduced to 16.5 minutes, climaxing with this paragraph: "True meaning reverberates in the unspoken chasm between what we can show and what we can tell about it. O.K., that's it for this Blink. But before we let you go, we wanted to let you know that this Blink was narrated by an A.I.-generated voice model. That's me." This is in place of Wittgenstein's arduously reached mystical conclusion, "What we cannot speak about we must pass over in silence."

2.

I think it was in the late seventies that I began to be suspicious about applying invasive medical technologies to a body in decline with low life expectancy. I suppose unconscious suspicions could have arisen when I was one year old and involuntarily had my adenoids and tonsils taken out at a military hospital while my father was in the navy during World War II. This did not help my respiratory issues and would not be done today.

As an adult, I first experienced excess interventions with my sister-in-law Lynne. She had a history of liver disease and respiratory ailments and was extremely underweight. When she was forty-two, as the liver disease became severe, a liver bypass was attempted to prolong her life. She went into a coma and died within a few days.

It seemed absurd to think that such a frail body could survive the procedure. Distracted by remedial hopes, neither she nor the family had a chance to come together in facing her terminal diagnosis. We had only reached the denial stage in the five stages of grief as Elisabeth Kübler-Ross articulated them in *On Death and Dying* (1969), a book we only read after Lynne's passing.

Within a year my father was diagnosed, at age sixty-seven, with stomach cancer. An operation was performed to remove the cancer. It was found to have spread to his lungs and could not be removed. He was stitched back up, eliminating his belly button, and died, as predicted, within two months. With him and in family gatherings, we were able to process the grief of his dying, and his passing was peaceful.

Shortly after his death, my mother, also in her late sixties, had a bowel obstruction and was diagnosed with colon cancer. A colostomy was performed. When the cancer was removed from the colon, it was found that it had spread to the liver and was inoperable there. She agreed to try an experimental chemo pump that might extend her life by two years. We had, it seemed then, too much time to process her prolonged decline and low quality of life, though she may not have felt that was the case. I think she hoped that her being a guinea pig might help others.

After these three deaths one after another, family mortality settled down. Our attention was taken up with our daughters' teen years. The AIDS mortality crisis was growing and people we knew were suffering and dying. Then in 1992 my husband had a heart attack. The doctor put him in twenty-four-hour intensive care, which felt to him like hell. After that, separated from us, he was in the hospital for a week while various tests and procedures were performed. He was thought to be out of danger. The attack was considered a wake-up call, requiring lifestyle changes but no further medical procedures. He died during a nap on the afternoon of his return. We had focused on lifestyle changes, not the stages of grief.

Around this time Sogyal Rinpoche's *The Tibetan Book of Living and Dying* came out. It very much spoke to my need. It also addressed the larger community of grief and disorientation from the AIDS crisis. My daughter and I heard the author give teachings in Boston. He began silently. His gaze moved as if from person to person, touching with peaceful attention, it seemed, each of us in the large auditorium. I was drawn to the kindly pragmatism of his Buddhist approach.

This approach is hard to describe. Gary Snyder makes an attempt in his poem "Avocado."

> The Dharma is like an avocado!...
>
> The great big round seed
> In the middle,
> Is your own Original Nature—...
>
> Hard and slippery,
> It looks like
> You should plant it—but then
> It shoots out thru the
> fingers—
> gets away.

The farther I wandered into dharma teachings and practices, the more I appreciated their subtle practicality. Things end up being just as they are. "First a bowl is a bowl, then a bowl is not a bowl, then a bowl is a bowl."

Dharma teachings are not metaphysical, theological, or ontological, the usual western philosophical domains of the subtle. This is an aspect of the way all western philosophy may be seen as a footnote to Plato.

Dharma teachings are psychological and ethical. They involve deep meditative attention to the mind's transient, elusive, and slippery stream.

The mind is found to be so subtle that, upon searching, one finds it not to be findable.

The mind's aggregates, enumerated as forms, feelings, concepts, residual impressions, and consciousness, are interdependent, constantly changing, empty of any permanent being of their own.

Buddha perceived and taught that the mindstream wanders, in its past births, during this life, and in its rebirths, through three realms including thirty-one planes of samsara. The journey is driven by the finite potencies of karma (previous actions of body, speech, and mind). When one potency is exhausted, another ripens. Even the most subtle mental realms achieved through meditation are planes of samsara, planes of impermanence and change.

In the sense-sphere or desire realm there are four negative birth and rebirth planes (hell, animals, hungry ghosts, and titans) and seven positive planes (humans and six heavenly gods planes).

The fine material or form realm has sixteen planes experienced through increasingly subtle meditation levels.

The formless immaterial realm includes four planes involving deepening levels of formless mental attainments.

Before Buddha achieved enlightenment, during his years of yoga austerities as a student of the yogis Kalama and Uddaka Rammaputta, he experienced the most subtle realms of samsara, the eighth meditative attainment (the fourth and deepest plane in the formless realm), beyond the experiences of infinite space, infinite consciousness, and nothingness.

He had experienced all the planes of samsara and still not found the knowledge he was seeking.

During his night of enlightenment, with his mind calm, concentrated, and imperturbable through his meditative attainments, he "directed it to the recollection of past lives" and attained "the first true knowledge." Next, he "directed it to knowledge of the passing away and rebirth of beings." He then "understood how beings fare on according to their actions, the second true knowledge." Directing his mind "to knowledge of the destruction of taints," he "directly knew as it actually is: This is suffering. This is the origin of suffering. This is the cessation of suffering. This is the way leading to the cessation of suffering." Likewise he knew the taints, their origin, their cessation, and the way to their cessation. His liberation from the taints of desire, samsaric existence, and ignorance was "the third knowledge."

For all of us unenlightened ones, these accounts of planes, realms, knowledges, etc. are artifices to be imagined, practical means for teaching us, thought-coverings empty of any inherent reality, fingers pointing to the moon, not the moon itself.

Buddha was at first reluctant to say anything. He had gone beyond the most subtle formless planes of samsara. How could he teach others the way to his experience? The gods of the desire realm convinced him that sentient beings needed his help. Then he found ways to show a path.

He called his teaching "the Dhamma by the middle," a middle way between the extremes of saying that things exist (essentialism) and things don't exist (nihilism), like the middle between inhaling and exhaling, between life and death, between samsara and nirvana.

3.

It is said that Buddha was a prince who had been protected from life's sufferings. Not until he was a young man did he see an old person, a sick person, and corpse. He was overwhelmed by these realities of life and left home in search of wisdom.

The wisdom he found begins with the truth that we humans in the desire realm tend to be obsessed with our desires and avoid thinking about suffering, disease, old age, and death unless they advance heavily upon us.

Although I had inevitably experienced sickness and loss in my life, it wasn't until I approached seventy that old age and life expectancy became conspicuous, although still mostly as numerical facts and social categories.

On my seventieth birthday, to give a spiritual meaning and direction to my old age, I took refuge and vowed the bodhisattva vow with my dharma teacher Khenpo Karthar Rinpoche, who was eighty-seven years old (a wise elder) and the abbot of Karma Triyana Dharmachakra monastery in Woodstock, NY.

The bodhisattva vow is an aspiration to be there for others, to be aware of others' suffering, and to avoid the extremes of either escaping to nirvanic bliss or drowning in samsaric suffering.

It assumes, as "useful means," an ethic of compassion and loving kindness embedded in an awareness that all dharmas, all phenomena, are empty, yet they appear. That awareness is one of those avocado pits that slip from grasping.

In Shantideva's classic eighth-century Mahayana text *A Guide to the Bodhisattva's Way of Life,* a bodhisattva aspires to cultivate generosity, carefulness, patience, effort, meditative stability, and wisdom. The first five address our emotional afflictions. Wisdom, the most subtle and difficult, addresses our cognitive obscurations.

Cognitive obscurations overlay an illusory real and abiding self onto the way we experience ourselves and others, all of whom are empty of such an abiding reality. When one realizes this wisdom, one begins to realize one's bodhisattva potential, and not merely to aspire to cultivate it.

The last verse and refrain from Leonard Cohen's song "Anthem" expresses this wisdom of emptiness, love, and refuge.

> You can add up the parts
> but you won't have the sum
> you can strike up the march,
> there is no drum.
> Every heart
> to love will come
> but like a refugee.
>
> Ring the bells that still can ring,
> Forget your perfect offering.
> There is a crack in everything.
> That's how the light gets in.

Cohen wrote this song in 1992 when he was fifty-eight years old. Subsequently he recorded the narration for a two-part *Tibetan Book of the Dead* documentary that came out in 1994, two years after Sogyal Rinpoche's *Tibetan Book of Living and Dying*. Cohen then spent 1994-1999 in retreat at Mount Baldy Zen Center in California.

The documentary narration begins, "Death is real. It comes without warning and it cannot be escaped." We are told that, while teachings about death and dying are now mostly lost in the west, they remain a part of daily life in Himalayan Buddhist cultures.

The documentary follows, in the first part, the forty-nine day reading of the eleventh chapter of the *Tibetan Book of the Dead* beside the body of a very old man and, in the second part, beside the body of a young family man. It is filmed in India in the Tibetan communities of Ladakh.

The English translations of the text are from the 1975 translation by Francesca Fremantle and Chögyam Trungpa. In the first part of the documentary, the lama who reads the text is accompanied by a young monk. Trungpa tells in his Foreword how he received the text transmission and began training in the teachings when he was eight years old. The training included visiting dying or dead people about four times a week. This way, he says, "the notion of impermanence becomes a living experience rather than a philosophical view."

Gyurme Dorje's translation of the complete fourteen-chapter text came out in 2005. There it is said that the lama reading the text "should be motivated by a sincere compassion for all living beings and should have mastered in his own mental continuum the direct experiential cultivation of the dying processes." His voice as he reads should be melodious and soothing.

I first became aware of the book through the 1927 W.Y. Evans-Wentz translation of the eleventh chapter, "The Great Liberation by Hearing." My edition included a 1939 "Psychological Commentary" by C.G. Jung.

The Tibetan title of the book is *Bardo Thödol,* literally translated as *The Great Liberation by Hearing in the Intermediate States.* It was composed in the eighth century by Guru Rinpoche Padmasambhava, the guru who helped bring Buddhism to Tibet. It distinguishes six intermediate states (bardos) in the circle of birth and death: waking, dream, meditation, death, luminosity (between death and rebirth), and rebirth.

The fourth chapter in the Gyurme Dorje translation, "The Introduction to Awareness: Natural Liberation through Naked Perception," is introduced by the editors as "the essence of the esoteric instruction by which the student is introduced to the ultimate nature of mind." This teaching, it says, "should be received from an accomplished lineage holder" for its philosophical view to be experientially cultivated. I have received this teaching in a separate form as Dzogchen and Mahamudra. I return to it as a resting place in my subtle wanderings.

The chapter, written and recited as poetry, points out that the various "classes of living beings discern phenomenal appearances in their differing ways: / Eternalistic extremists [and others] who are remote from [the Buddhist perspective] perceive [appearances] in terms of a dichotomy of eternalism and nihilism." Perennial Philosophy is at the eternalist extreme, while contemporary technology tends toward the nihilist extreme.

After citing various other differing ways of apprehension, it concludes that "bewilderment comes about through attachment to these respective [views]. / Yet, even though all those appearances, of which one is aware in one's mind, / Do arise as discernible manifestations, / Buddhahood is present [simply] when they are not subjectively apprehended or grasped. / Bewilderment...comes about through their subjective apprehension."

The problem is attachment, the subjective grasp that distorts the clarity of the way things, including ideas and views, appear.

The eleventh chapter, "The Great Liberation," addresses the confused projections of karma, the unconscious tendencies that generate peaceful and wrathful mental images in the luminosity bardo. (They are also familiar to us in the dream bardo). The instruction is "simply to recognize them as your projections," as the self-display of awareness. Don't attach to them.

C. G. Jung's commentary on "The Great Liberation" focuses on these images as "the data of psychic experience," "the archetypal contents of the unconscious." They are "analogous to Plato's forms" as "categories of the imagination" and "organs of the pre-rational psyche." He terms the layer of unconscious psyche made up of these forms the collective unconscious.

The images, symbolism, and iconography of "The Great Liberation" are based on a sixth-century Indian Buddhist tantric compilation, *Guhyagarbha Tantra.* In the form of a visualized mandala circle, it maps our natural spectrum of mundane psychological states with a view to naturally purifying them. Tantric practices are said to be so powerful that they enable us to achieve liberation from our bewildered wanderings in one lifetime.

As interesting as these tantric practices are, I relate more to the philosophies and practices for investigating the nature of mind. However, I did buy one iconographic thangka painting when I was in Dharamsala. It hangs above my desk and depicts the union of the primordial male and female Buddhas, Samantabhadra and Samantabhadri. Hanging next to it is a Shriyantra I myself painted, depicting a similar yogic union of male and female energies in the form of intertwined upward and downward triangles.

In reciting "The Great Liberation," after respiration has ceased, the reader introduces the images of Samantabhadri and Samantabhadra in union. Colored white, she is conscious awareness as emptiness. Colored blue, he is conscious awareness as radiant, brilliant, and vibrant. They are naked, seated in yab-yum (father-mother) union on a moon disk, sun disk, and lotus rising from a pool of water in a pale green field. There they are, above my desk, in a corner of my study, having wandered there all the way from a thangka shop in Dharamsala and my pre-rational psyche.

Tattoos

He seems more other than the rest of us
in our monastic or sober lay costumes:
owl-large glasses framed in flaming red,
full-bodied soft skin blushing pink
through a dark blue thicket of tattoos
under a tropic tangerine shirt in the Buddha room
as we learn to cut through our demons,
solid notions of self and other,
to the slow drone of a two-headed drum.

At supper I remark on his tattoos.
They commemorate, he tells me,
his battles against cancer and HIV.
For twenty years now he has won them.
He extends the practices he has learned
to cut through the demons of others,
their diseases, their addictions, feeding them,
exchanging self and other,
the dense skin-sewn pattern of his design
a reminder from the world of dreams
that demons are not different as illusions
from mind's rituals that heal them.

I tell of my daughter, how a cancer diagnosis
made her want to be blessed with tattoos,
to feel their art would live with her body,
that the demons of fear would be cut through.
Now she too is well, soft skin blushing pink,
scarred but whole.

Perspectives

1.

In the suburb of Milwaukee where I grew up, we lived a short walk away from a bluff overlooking Lake Michigan. Gazing eastward from the bluff toward the unseen further shore, I contemplated the vast rippling deep while the waves' rhythmic pulse pounded on the rocks below. Sometimes I would go down the steep stone steps to touch the water as it washed back and forth over a narrow beach of shiny pebbles and stones during low tide, or to contemplate more intimately the water's dark heavy surge during high tide. Sometimes my focus wandered to the unseen beyond the horizon.

In Patañjali's classic definition, "Yoga is the restraint of the mind's waves. Then the seer sees his own form. Otherwise he sees the waves' form." The mind can concentrate on the movement of the waves or on the whole deep-breathing body of water. In the Great Vehicle Buddhist view, the water and its waves are not separate, the mind and its waves are not separate. This corroborated the teaching of the lake that had impressed itself on my mind.

A passage in Lucretius's poem *On the Nature of Things* aroused these reflections. He is trying to convince the reader to take a holistic view, a view with sufficient space and distance to peacefully regard material motion. Correspondences from sense experience, he argues, show how "the sum total seems to abide in supreme quietude." Woolly sheep and frolicsome lambs wander off to more dewy high pastures until all we can see is a green hill dappled with fleecy whiteness. In military maneuvers, the gleam of legions clothed in bronze, the thunder of tramping feet and galloping horsemen, when seen and heard from a mountain above, become a calm glow and hum resting on a plain. (2.308-332)

Auden's poem "Musée des Beaux Arts" was written in 1940 when it was hard to find a sufficiently distant place, other than the arts or prayer, to view the metallic gleams of war. Auden addresses our human perspective as intimated in paintings where the miraculous birth, the dreadful martyrdom, the boy Icarus falling out of the sky happen unnoticed in the background.

About suffering they were never wrong,
The Old Masters: how well they understood
Its human position; how it takes place
While someone else is eating or opening a window or just walking dully
    along,...

Denise Levertov's poem, "The Showings: Lady Julian of Norwich, 1342-1416," written in the 1980s, wonders at the holy mysteries shown to Julian, who "lived in dark times, as we do." Julian received a vision of Christ holding our dark world, the size of a hazelnut, safe in his pierced hand. "She was shown the knowledge: *Love was his meaning.*"

Our high-tech telescopes, spaceships, satellites, and rockets have replaced mountaintops and hills as places of spacious human viewpoint. Meanwhile we are cluttering not only Mt. Everest and the deep ocean but space itself with our debris. And yet it has perhaps always been true that, for living beings, the journey to the deep places of our inner space, not the distant view, corresponds to the spacious perspective of Lucretius's philosophical quietude. He rejected religion because it aroused fear and superstition rather than love and knowledge. Our inner spaces too become cluttered. X-rays and MRIs show us only the tangible things to be feared.

In Caspar David Friedrich's painting "The Wanderer above a Sea of Mist," the wanderer's form, seen from behind, and the rocky peak on which he stands, are defined and finite in the foreground while the wanderer contemplates the vast space unfolding beyond where he is. His gaze is slightly down towards the crag-pierced mist sea, not across or upward toward the quiet sky beyond.

In "Chalk Cliffs on Rügen," painted during Friedrich's honeymoon, a woman and two men, their backs to the viewer, gaze down from a dark edge over the luminous white cliffs and calm blue sea below. We viewers, like the figures in Friedrich's paintings, have our faces turned away as we strive to see beyond our finitude, beyond our baggage. The paintings reflect a vision, sometimes misted, sometimes luminous, sometimes dark, within the artist and within us, like when I gazed across Lake Michigan.

For the last twenty years or so, Lake Awosting in the Shawangunks has been my preferred pilgrimage place for the contemplation of stones and water. I have humanized the scale of my reverie site to a body of water in which I can immerse myself and, circumambulating, view from the varying perspectives of its bounds, some low shorelines, some high cliffs, some wooded slopes, some marsh. It is nature's version of the way, in India, one circumambulates a temple and then enters its *garbhagriha,* its womb home, a way that had roots in mountain and water pilgrimages.

It was long my ambition to circumambulate Mount Kailash and dip in Mansarovar, the glacial lake beside it, sacred to Hindus, Jains, Buddhists, and the indigenous Tibetan Bonpo. Buddhists regard Kailash as the navel of the universe. Hindus and yogis consider it the home of Shiva, the yoga lord. The site is now in the Tibet Autonomous Region of China. The pilgrimage involves a rigorous journey by bus and foot.

A few years ago, my years having accrued to well past three score and ten, I had to turn back from an attempted trek to a different Himalayan holy lake, Mahinamesh, below Mount Mahinamesh Kailas. Part way up, I realized my legs were not up to the climb, sat down beside the stony trail, and sobbed as if I had just suffered a great loss, a loss I only afterwards saw as an abjuration of ambition, determination, and striving. And yet it felt in part like a sobbing of release and purification, of accepting a less lofty perspective on life, a hedonistic calculus of the ratio of pleasure to pain.

My German heritage, as I experienced it, involved a Faustian culture of *streben*, a driven approach to life that forgoes cultivating a patient intuition of relatedness. I think of this problem as my German heritage, but we humans and living beings of all kinds have the potential to isolate our wills, exceed our vital scale, and self-destruct. We gaze over an abyss projected from the restlessness habituated within us.

As Rome was moving toward Empire, Lucretius committed himself to the rural scene and a quiet philosophy developed in an exurban garden. He delights in describing, with idyllic pastoral examples, how natural things, through their differences, relate to one another, like a mother cow to her calf, or a ewe to her lamb. Buddha, more radically, left the court and became a yogi in the forest. I'm not up for going that far. An exurban garden is a nice middle way.

I sit here in my study overlooking my balcony peopled with pollinator plants, herbs, flowers, and vegetables: snapdragons, zinnias, roses, anise hyssop, nasturtiums, valerian, bronze fennel, dahlias, lemon verbena, a bay tree, white myrtle, orange mint, jasmine, summer savory, golden sage, thyme, basil, arugula, chard, green beans, golden beets, buckwheat, and a hanging fuchsia attractive to humming birds, whose first visit of the season was yesterday. Over the balcony edge I can see the crowns of trees, from my linden tree nearby offering perches to songbirds, to the neighbors' trees and a small woods at the bottom of the hill. A balmy scent comes in with the breeze through the screen door.

This is the second year I've given up my plot in the local community garden which was too far away for me to tend it well. It's the first year I've set up a balcony vegetable patch using large rectangular grow bags. The carrot and lettuce seeds didn't sprout at all, and the Russian kale is full of holes from slugs. Everything else is doing well so far. A very hot summer is predicted. Already June has been the hottest ever, so I need to water diligently. At dawn and dusk I check for weeds and each plant's needs. I am oddly content with the small intimacy of this task.

2.

On my first trip to India in 1984 a Vedic pandit heard that I was studying Sanskrit and yoga. He asked me the meaning of an Upanishadic epigraph in Sanskrit:

> OM purnam adah purnam idam / purnat purnam udacyate /
> purnasya purnam adaya / purnam evavashishyate.
>
> [All this is full. All that is full. / From fullness, fullness comes. /
> Fullness taken from fullness, / fullness remains.]

I was familiar with the epigraph and told him how I pictured fullness in holistic terms as the vastness of the universe. No, he said, its meaning is as of a seed. His view was microcosmic and psychological, rooted in yoga meditation and seeing the seed of fullness in the heart. My view was macrocosmic and metaphysical, rooted in the prayer imagery of the Psalms and hymns derived from them. Unlike his view, mine was in some way, as I pictured it, external to myself, looking beyond myself.

Through the study and practice of yoga and its philosophy, my perspective found itself shifting from far to near, from outside to inside. After some years, I began to study and practice Buddhist meditation wherein awareness is fluid between external and internal perspectives. It is done with eyes open. It lets go of the division between self and other. It leads, as the Middle Way Buddhist philosopher Nagarjuna concludes, to appreciation that Buddha, "out of compassion, / taught the true dharma for the abandonment of all views."

The gurus of the Vedic Upanishads taught meditations for experiencing the oneness of Atman (the Self, seed of fullness in the heart) and Brahman (the Universal Spirit). Buddha found attachment to this view to be an obstacle to experiencing the transitory and interdependent nature of all phenomena. He developed and taught a deep-looking meditation practice that sees emptiness, a lack of inherent being, as the way things are. Our suffering, he said, comes from how we solidify our experiences, not opening to the in-between spaces, the empty gaps in the mindstream between sensations, feelings, and thoughts arising and passing away.

The Prologue to the book *Void and Fullness in the Buddhist, Hindu and Christian Traditions,* a collection of papers presented at an interreligious seminar in Sarnath, India in 1999, directs attention to emptiness and fullness as shared spiritual experiences. It cites the "Wisdom in Emptiness" dialogue between D. T. Suzuki and Thomas Merton, where Zen and Christian spiritual practices involve a striving "after innocence, emptiness." It also cites Swami Abhishiktananda's dialogue, in his diary and his life, between his Christian devotion and the non-duality of the Upanishads. He writes, "I am Fullness, *purnam,* precisely in this letting-go of myself everywhere."

I was first drawn to India because of its long history of interfaith dialogue. In the ancient Vedas (Rig Veda I.166.46) it is said, *Ekam sat, vipra bahuda vadanti* [truth is one, experiencers speak of it in many ways]. By way of communication, we give names and forms to our spiritual experiences. These cultural conventions can become disconnected from the direct personal experiences that evoked them. Buddhists have the sayings that the finger pointing to the moon is not the moon, and that there are eighty-four thousand doors to truth and we only need to pass through one of them.

Since 2014 India has been ruled by a Hindu-centric man and a right-wing Hindu nationalist perspective hostile to non-Indic faiths, distorting their own tradition. Here in America, despite the First Amendment mandating freedom of religion in America, the Christian right aspires to impose its perspective on everyone. And yet here I am sitting at my desk, trusting the law of impermanence, somewhat calming my mind by playing with words, enjoying the plants on my balcony, keeping my accounts, reading Lucretius II.1 as he tells Memmius, "Nothing is more blissful than to occupy the heights effectively fortified by the teachings of the wise, tranquil sanctuaries" from the games of intellectual eminence, wealth, rank, and power.

Close Accounts

My father-in-law was a CPA given to precision
and regularity of habit.
He taught me to keep close accounts
on a Boorum and Pease work pad.

He planted snapdragons in a narrow strip
between his house and his driveway.
He cut the flowers on short stems
to fit his dinner table slotted bowl.

Our Milwaukee reunions took place yearly
around his August 10th birthday.
He liked to have roast pork, sauerkraut,
potatoes, cantaloupe à la mode.

His precision was usually quiet and helpful.
He promptly cleaned all spills
and maintained both silver
and shoes in a polished condition.

At UWis he learned to run in cross country
instead of ROTC teaching him to fight.
He quit a job that required fixing books.
Bent by arthritis, he honed moral fiber.

He blessed food to our use and us to service.
He went to church every Sunday.
When I asked for his rule of life
he recited "Invictus."

Nearing ninety, when he was dying, he felt
God near, comforting him in his room.

It never occurred to him before, he said,
that religion was about something real.

I thought of him fondly today as I planted
snapdragons in a window box
and kept household accounts
on a Boorum and Pease work pad.

Wholes, Fragments, Erasures, and Bubbles

1.

My enjoyment of Lucretius's Epicurean poem in praise of the nature of things led me to investigate the historical epic of his predecessor Ennius (239-169 BCE), known for his absorption and transferring of Greek language and culture into Latin, considered to be Lucretius's archaic Latin model.

It turns out that Ennius's work, like so many ancient works, is only available in discontinuous small fragments. The longest fragment is from Augustine, *City of God* II.21, quoting Cicero quoting Ennius, "On manners and on men of good old time stands firm the Roman state."

Augustine goes on to quote Cicero in his own words. "That line for its conciseness and truth sounds to me like the utterance of an oracle...Our own generation inherited the republic, an exquisite masterpiece, indeed, though faded with age, but it failed to restore its original colors."

I like the way Lucretius, like Buddha and nature-based Indigenous traditions and unlike history-based Augustine and Cicero, sees flourishing and decline as ongoing and inevitable cycles in the nature of things. When we grumble about our degenerate times, he says, we fail to "comprehend that all things gradually decay and go to the reef of destruction, outworn by the ancient lapse of years." (II.1173-1174)

Certainly of late some of us including me have been grumbling about our times even as we struggle to comprehend our own decay of body and mind and the decay of our loved ones. How to articulate the loss and incomplete recovery of our words and thought fragments, the discontinuities of mortality? Is this handicap why, in old age, I resort to short paragraphs, collaging others' thoughts, recording bits and pieces?

As so many of us bury ourselves in our screens and media addictions and google for more and more bits of info that have slipped from our memory, it can feel like we are replacing ourselves with technology. Yet to come is the full impact of AI with its superhuman collection of data. Like the fragments buried in the rubbish mounds in Oxyrhynchus, the Dead Sea scrolls, or the books in the Villa of the Papyri buried and carbonized by Vesuvius, data banks are becoming our storehouse of learning, seemingly less mortal than we are. Meanwhile we are passing on to our descendants a broken world, nature altered by humans to an unprecedented degree.

2.

Years ago Gabbie, my first grandchild, when she was very young, maybe two or three, cried unconsolably when her cookie broke. As she held the two pieces apart, one in each hand, she kept saying, through her sobs, "It will never be whole again." She wanted to bite into it when it was whole.

Her crying was like an oracle of her future difficulties with life and her inability to find wholeness. Now twenty-seven, she continues to occupy a piece of my mind outside the pedagogical reaches of Plato, Lucretius, or Buddha.

Gabbie's mother, my daughter Sarah, when she was growing up, used to say that our family lived in a bubble. To the bubble of a moderately comfortable middle-class life in the liberal NYC metropolitan area we added, with our practices of yoga and meditation, the bubble of an ashram and, with our attention to classical literature, the bubble of an ivory tower or scriptorium engaged with the keep of old learning. Distanced from these bubbles, which I still occupy, she is now on a mission, as she says, teaching literacy to students from an impoverished Ojibway reservation in northern Wisconsin while keeping her broken, part Native family there together as best she can.

In the 2003 Korean Zen film *Spring Summer Fall Winter Spring,* a young boy ties stones onto a frog, a fish, and a snake. Unseen, the Zen master watches him doing this. While the boy is sleeping, the master ties a stone onto his back. When the boy wakes up and feels pain from the stone, the Zen master reminds him of the pain he caused the animals. Release them, he says, but if any of them has died, you will carry that stone for the rest of your life.

The fish has died and the boy buries it. He releases the frog, but when he finds the snake dead, he holds the dead snake tied to the fatal stone and sobs saturated with grief like my grandson sobbed over his cookie. The movie follows his slow ultimately liberating journey through the stages of life carrying the burden of that metaphorical stone.

Gabbie was a sensitive child and things were not stable in her household. As the years went by, some deep weight of sadness never seemed to leave her, perhaps an inheritance of depression in the family. Also she is half Ojibway, with the patrimony of a broken cultural heritage and inherited trauma.

Just before puberty she began to acquire risky manic behaviors. These self-medicative actions got riskier and riskier until their neurological damages evolved into seizures and sometimes violent psychotic paranoid episodes in her mid-twenties. At the time I am writing this, she is in jail, her fifth incarceration. It has not been determined whether to give a bipolar or schizophrenic diagnosis with medications that might help her.

When she was twenty-five she began to identify as a trans woman. Until then, I knew her as Gabriel or Gabe and experienced her as an unquestionably male grandson. Her favorite early book, which she memorized, was *Drummer Hof,* about seven soldiers making a cannon. She loved to say the culminating lines, "Drummer Hof fired it off." I have difficulty using the female pronoun as I tell of those pre-trans years.

Lucretius describes how nature orders processes of both thriving and degeneration. When a blow greater than nature can endure strikes in any living being, the vital knots of the soul are unloosed, ejected, and dispersed. But if the blow is less violent, the remaining vital motions prevail, quiet the torment of the blow, and call everything back into accustomed channels. (II.944ff)

The vital knots of Gabbie's soul seem to have been repeatedly ejected and called back, frayed and tangled, with missing parts, the vital motions prevailing with damage. It is hard to imagine that she will journey through all the stages of life or find a path toward liberation from her psychological and neurodivergent problems and burden of pain.

When she was younger, I felt she was most whole when she was fly fishing. She attuned her mind and body to the stream. Her motion became fluid like a fish. When she caught a fish, she caressed it and spoke to it before gently releasing it back into the water. (In Ojibway culture, fishes are people.) Fish learn from this, she said. But she herself seems to have a more dominating compulsion to immerse herself in brokenness as if to learn from it.

3.

My daughter Anna's friends Matthea Harvey, a poet, and Amy Jean Porter, an artist, collaborated on an erasure poetry book, *Of Lamb.* Inspired by Tom Phillips's *A Humument,* deconstructed from a Victorian novel, Matthea resolved to buy and make an erasure project of the first book she found for three dollars. It turned out to be David Cecil's *A Portrait of Charles Lamb.*

She whited out all but a few words per page, among which, on almost every page, were Charles's name and the name of Mary, his sister. A poem emerged as a variation on the nursery rhyme "Mary Had a little Lamb" shadowed by the mental health issues of the Lamb family and particularly of Mary. Amy Jean created paintings for each page.

The narrative assumes that we know something of Charles's lamblike personality and his relationship with his sister, that there was a history of mental health issues in their family, and that, in Mary's first psychotic episode, she stabbed her mother to death. After that, Charles cared for her while she relapsed repeatedly. Without going into these factual details, Matthea suggests them with these words drawn from Cecil's book: "Lamb on his side, / gasping, / Poor Lamb! // Nerves his family, / Trouble his home, / Dark Spirits his company."

I was moved by *Of Lamb* when it came out in 2011 and I first read it. At that time Sarah and her family were living with me. Gabbie was fourteen. Her dark shadows seemed mostly depressive. We could not foresee that, in 2023, in a paranoid psychotic episode, she would attack her father.

In 2021 she went through a period of sending me essays. I think it was in response to my sending her Noah Levine's *Refuse Recovery: A Buddhist Path to Recovering from Addiction,* which includes a written practice, and her own discovery of Allison Hawthorne Deming's *Zoologies: On Animals and the Human Spirit.* Deming's book spoke to Gabbie's alienation from and critique of the dominant culture as well as her efforts to integrate, in expressing her identity, the Native American and European sides of her heritage.

At the beginning of one of the essays, "Generational Defiance," she writes, "As a slight forward I'd like to say, among the men in my blood line, at least those that I've known while alive, I've made the worst choices possible while being given the best situation out of them all. I feel as if my hands are stained with guilt, at least that's how it feels."

She goes on to say that "it's part of my duty to tell what I know of the three generations of men who came before me, and how their scars and trauma affected the next, and how I've observed, felt, and tried, often failing with near fatal consequences, to break free of the emotional scarring and dark memories that seem almost etched into my DNA."

I reread these words now when Gabbie has come to identify as a trans Native woman, still making bad choices, still wanting to break free, to tell what she knows. Sometimes it seems like what's whited out leaves only the scars and the trauma, the deepening ruts.

For a while when she was in jail in Minneapolis I sent her weekly letters by snail mail. I wrote about ordinary homey things like my balcony garden or baking bread, much the way my grandma wrote to me when I was in college.

I hoped she would be able to write back to me, to capture some of her thoughts onto paper, to befriend herself in this way.

Writing a snail mail letter felt in itself somewhat healing. It would journey whole, in its enveloped form of paper with ink-scripted words, touched by my hands, from New York to Minneapolis. An email on the other hand is deconstructed and reassembled like the way, on *Star Trek*, Scottie beamed people's bodies up, or the way Lester, Gabbie's paternal grandfather, came to hope that his body would be raised from the grave.

Lester was Gabbie's predecessor in drug and alcohol addiction and psychotic delusion. All his life he was terrified of dying. He had visions of hell and was convinced he would burn there. In his seventies, when he was near death, he did not want his body to be cremated. He wanted it to be buried whole. It was a heavy body. Gabbie, with her brother and father, carried it whole to the grave. They did not mark the grave.

In response to my snail mails, I received an envelope with a card and four pages of yellow legal paper, three of them torn fragments, "poems and phrases from jail." On one of the torn pages is this short poem:

if only I was
an angel not the other, I'd be healthy
even alone.

The untorn page has a poem about the desire to go for a walk on a cool spring morning. Here is the second half of the poem:

...bluegill
and bass thrown back into water turned
murky with runoff, a need for dreams, and
time fulfilled at peace with a body

in growing pains, painfully
growing away from self.

but a fractured bone heals, a limb
snapped still buds, and as spring
ends my roots pull from a pool of water far from sight, and I flower
to heal with scents engraved
on a supposedly damaged brain

Should she be released from jail on parole, she will have no place to stay, no job she will be able to keep. She does not acknowledge her mental disease or seek treatment for it. This lack of insight, I read, is part of the disease.

Despairing of finding a pragmatic solution, I turn in my bewilderment to a Native American Mojave poet, Natalie Diaz. Her poem "When My Brother Was an Aztec," in her collection with this title and this theme, recounts the burden of her wayward and delusionary brother on her family. "They didn't know / what else to do except be there to pick him up when he died.... My brother...broke them to pieces." What else is there to do but love wholly and be powerless?

4.

Outside of my cultivated bubble, on a forest path, beside a lake or stream where nothing speaks in words, the rippling water, the markings on bark, the patterns of butterfly and bird flights, the whisperings of a breeze in leaves, the shifting shapes of clouds, the lichen on stones, every detail has its eloquence.

I grew up in Wisconsin and spent every summer of my adolescent years canoeing on lakes and streams in the Northwoods, the world through which, before colonization, the Ojibway travelled by foot and canoe.

Their favorite stories were of the follies of their half human, half spirit folk hero Nana'b'oozoo. He embodies humans' tendency to blunder impulsively without listening to reason or the advice of their elders, who include the whole natural world that appeared before we did.

He was raised by N'okomiss, his grandmother, the archetypal teacher and guardian of knowledge, whose teachings he repeatedly fails to follow, only to return to her for comfort and guidance. From her he eventually learns the Ojibway heritage and teaches it to the people. A final story tells how the Ojibway took up the colonizers' ways, abandoned their heritage, and repudiated him. He paddled off and disappeared in a canoe with his grandmother.

Humans are said to be composed of a physical part and a soul-spirit with a capacity to dream and receive visions. Because of our moral blundering, it is hard for us to keep our visions from breaking as we move through life's stages. Time and time again, up to seven times, we may digress from the path and find our way back. Nowadays, as for Gabbie, the sacred search for a vision at puberty, guided by an elder, has given way to abuse of alcohol and drugs. A spirit of excess, Weendigo, takes hold of anyone losing moderation. Both the legal and the illegal forces of consumer capitalism, including the drug markets, are modern weendigoes lying in wait to devour us.

Basil Johnston's books *Ojibway Heritage* (1976) and *The Manitous: The Spiritual World of the Ojibway* (1995) were written to encourage Ojibways to learn about their traditions and recover their previously oral heritage. But

Johnston knows that reading a book is not enough. He reminds us that "the truths must be lived out and become part of the being of a person." Lucretius similarly reminds Memmius, the recipient of his opus, that reading it is not enough.

I take a walk in the woods and retreat to my bubble to write Gabbie a letter. Two weeks later it comes back from the jail unopened, stamped "Return to Sender / Not Here."

A little more than a year later, a few weeks before her twenty-eighth birthday, after she was in solitary confinement for almost four months in a different jail, there was a hearing where the judge determined that Gabbie was not mentally competent to make a decision on a plea bargain. He sent her to the state's Mental Health Institute for treatment. By her choice she is in the women's ward. She can receive books, food, and clothes. She requests protein powder and candy and tinted moisturizer.

Looking East at Day's Darkening

Across the water and the woods with its fallen leaves
and the sky with its clouds like thick porridge
shapes recede in waning light.

The silhouette of a raptor soars and descends
folding its wingspan onto the silhouette of a tree.

A stag flaunts his antler candelabra lit with power
then disappears in the tangled forest up a hill
where the trace of a late-grazing doe moves amid shadows.

Longevity, Food, and the Science of Mind

1.

Maria Branyas Morera, the world's oldest living person, recently died. She was 117 years and 168 days old. She told Guinness World Records that, besides luck and genetics, she owed her long life to "order, tranquility, good connection with family and friends, contact with nature, emotional stability, no worries, no regrets, lots of positivity, and staying away from toxic people."

I'm not sure what I think about longevity. Hard to imagine life without worries, although perhaps one gradually gives up on worrying. For now, I worry about, among other things, living too long, not in years but by less quantifiable measures such as well-being. After turning 80, I could no longer pretend I wasn't all that old. Being a practical and pro-active person, welcoming discipline, I collected a bunch of articles and books on warding off decline.

In a *New York Times* article, "The 7 Keys to Longevity," geriatricians offered me this evidence-based advice: move more, eat more fruits and vegetables, get enough sleep, don't smoke and don't drink too much, manage your chronic conditions (which usually are hypertension, high cholesterol, and pre-diabetes), prioritize your relationships, and cultivate a positive mind-set. It reminded me of writing the day's tasks on a whiteboard by the kitchen table when the children were more or less being trained to do them.

Cultivating a positive mind-set seems to be the key to all the keys in the testimonies of the record-holders. I did not feel I had a sufficiently positive mind-set about wrinkles, joint creaks, and the worst that might come.

My doctor recommended *How Not To Die: Discover the Foods Scientifically Proven To Prevent and Reverse Disease* (2015), by Michael Greger, MD, featuring Dr. Greger's Daily Dozen, which includes the usual recommendations to eat legumes, fruits (especially berries), vegetables (especially crucifers and greens), flaxseeds, nuts, spices, and whole grains, and to exercise. My doctor had added a nutrition degree to her medical degree because she had come to believe that most of the medical conditions she treated in her patients could have been prevented by changes in their diet and lifestyle. She has stopped practicing in order to teach these preventive measures to the young.

I was an almost model patient, something of a health nut since my thirties (that was when I began trying alternative approaches to asthma) and a vegetarian since my fifties (that was when my high cholesterol husband died of a heart attack). Now my doctor wanted me to refine this by eating more beans, nuts, and seeds and less dairy and to replace sweetened desserts with fresh fruits and nuts. I dutifully obeyed.

Meanwhile I subscribed to email newsletters from Blue Zones, the group founded by Dan Buettner and popularized in his 2008 book *The Blue Zones: Lessons for Living Longer from People Who've Lived the Longest,* profiling the diet and lifestyles of the remarkably long-lived residents of the Greek island of Ikaria, Okinawa in Japan, Ogliastra in Sardinia, Nicoya Peninsula in Costa Rica, and the Seventh-day Adventists of Loma Linda, California. Their diets are mostly drawn from local plants. They live in close community with one another, so they don't experience the social isolation that I fear with age. As part of their social life, the Ikarians enjoy local wine together and, as they say, they are so relaxed, they forget to die. The Adventists on the other hand are communally sober. My doctor, who was Italian, gave me the green light on a glass of red wine at dinner.

I also read Dean and Ayesha Sherzai's *The 30-Day Alzheimer's Solution: The Definitive Food and Lifestyle Guide to Preventing Cognitive Decline* (2021), involving the NEURO Plan, of which the five prongs are "Nutrition, Exercise, Unwind, Restorative Sleep, and Optimizing Cognitive Activity." They gave me two more dietary lists. Their NEURO 9 includes green leafy vegetables, whole grains, seeds, beans, nuts, crucifers, berries, herbs and spices, and tea, to which their Thoughtful 20 adds mushrooms, beets, avocados, olives, sweet potatoes, cacao, soy, brussels sprouts, and goji berries, and specifies quinoa and oats for the whole grains. No dairy, no honey, no wine. I began to fall back on the ancient wisdom, *carpe diem.*

As the number of us old folks keeps growing, so does the number of longevity techniques and books, some of them fearsome. Valter Longo's 2018 *The Longevity Diet: Discover the New Science Behind Stem Cell Activation and*

Regeneration to Slow Aging, Fight Disease, and Optimize Weight, offers a scientifically engineered fasting-mimicking diet (the FMD) to be done three to four times a year. Dr. Greger's 2023 sequel to *How Not To Die* is *How Not To Age.* It offers an Anti-Aging Eight that includes nuts, greens, berries, prebiotics and postbiotics, caloric restriction, protein restriction, NAD+, and xenohormesis and micro RNA manipulation. Having no idea what half of that means, I decided to apply Michael Pollan's seven-word food rule: "Eat Food. Not too much. Mostly plants."

I started baking wholegrain seeded sourdough bread following Mark Bittman's guidance in *Bittman Bread* (2021), and now I eat whatever, cooked in the Mediterranean style, goes nicely with my daily bread.

2.

For many years I taught a course on Approaches to Well-Being in Indo-Tibetan Traditions. Now that I am retired, I miss teaching it. In the course we explored classical Yoga philosophy and practice by reading the *Yogasutras* of Patañjali (ca 500-200 BCE). Then we learned about Samkhya philosophy, Yoga's theoretical counterpart. We also examined Ayurveda, the ancient Indian Science of Life, and its dietary recommendations.

Aside from their differences, there are many parallels between Samkhya-Yoga, Buddhist philosophy, and the Jain teachings I learned from my first meditation guru, as well as between Ayurveda and Tibetan Buddhist medicine. They are all based on practices of meditation connecting bodily and elemental sensory experience with increasingly subtle experiences of consciousness. These traditions inform my personal philosophy and daily practice, and they formed the holistic weave of the course.

Ayurveda analyzes the relationship among three humors (*doshas*) that characterize our mental/physical/spiritual constitution: *vata* (wind), *pitta* (bile), *kapha* (phlegm). Disease results when one becomes imbalanced and excessively dominates over the others. To moderate the imbalance, Ayurveda tailors dietary and lifestyle recommendations to the individual, season, time of life, and time of day. For example, most people as they age tend toward an imbalance of the *vata* humor. It particularly affects bodily hollows like bowels, joints, and respiratory organs. People like myself with excess *vata* do well with heavy, moist, heated food and not well with light, dry, cold food. To find out what foods and dishes aggravate, balance, or are neutral to my windy *vata* constitution, I consult books such as *The Ayurvedic Cookbook* by Amadea Morningstar with Urmila Desai (1990).

For all constitutions, Ayurveda recommends that we eat heated, unctuous, properly combined food in moderation when hungry, eat alone or with congenial people in a pleasant quiet place and with concentration, and feel gratitude and appreciation for what will become part of our body. It is also said that food should feed all five senses. It should look good, taste good, and smell good, and the process of eating should sound pleasing. For touch, it's recommended to eat with your hand, enjoying the food's textures. Since I live alone, I've gotten in the habit of eating more food with my hand, which is embarrassing when I have an opportunity to follow the Blue Zones guideline of eating with others.

Ayurveda analyzes foods by tastes and qualities which relate to our humors and to the way yoga analyzes our body and our mind. For example, the elements air and ether correspond with the humor *vata*, "the mover," which corresponds with the sensory experiences of hearing and touching, with emotions of attraction and desire, and the subtle energy *prana* (wind). The element fire corresponds with the humor *pitta*, "the digester and transformer," which corresponds with the sensory experience of seeing, emotions of aversion, and the subtle energy *tejas* (radiance). The elements water and earth correspond with the humor *kapha*, "the inherer," which corresponds with the sensory experiences of tasting and smelling and emotions of inattention, and the subtle energy *ojas* (love and cohesion). Samadhi, a goal of meditation, brings about balance and equilibrium among all these and other energies from subtle to gross and gross to subtle.

We learned about analyzing foods by their *rasa* (their taste on the tongue), *virya* (the hot or cold experience as they are swallowed into the stomach), and *vipak* (their experience after digestion), and about the six *rasas* (tastes), each related to specific elements: sweet (earth-water), sour (earth-fire), salty (water-fire), pungent (fire-air), bitter (air-ether), astringent (air-earth). This analysis becomes the basis of food recommendations for individual constitutions in seasonal and other circumstances. In my case, with a *vata*-dominant constitution, in *vata*-dominant old age, now approaching the *vata*-dominant dry windy season of autumn, I feel more ruffled and allergic and stay closer to the recommended lists, which help settle me down. Even among students of college age, there was usually a predominance of *vata*-dominant constitutions. This tendency is driven by our high-speed electronic and fast food lifestyle which often ruffles and ungrounds us and creates windy temperaments.

Dr. Vasant Lad's *Ayurveda: The Science of Self-Healing* (1984) is a book I used to put on my syllabus. At the beginning of the chapter on longevity he writes, "From the time of physical birth until physical death, the body is engaged in a continuous struggle against the aging process." He goes on to say, "On a deeper level, to combat aging it is necessary to balance the three subtle essences within the body: *prana, ojas, tejas....* Proper diet, exercise and lifestyle can create a balance among these three subtle essences, ensuring long life."

Robert Svoboda, in *Ayurveda: Life, Health and Longevity* (1992), affirms, "A human being is a space that is by nature unstable, perpetually prone to fall into disorder." These natural imbalances begin in the subtlest agitations of the mind. This is where yoga practice comes in. In *Yogasutras,* Patañjali defines yoga as "the restraint of the mind's waves." It teaches that the nature of the mind, unobscured by the waves, is clear consciousness. Usually what we experience is the instability of the churning waves.

To calm the churn, yoga practice moves from more outward to ever more inward restraints. It begins with five moral restraints (e.g., non-violence and truthfulness), followed by five observances (e.g., cleanliness and contentment). These are followed, in order, by restraints of posture, breath, and attention, and then by three ever-deepening concentrations of the mind. In deepest meditation, the mind sees itself unobscured by waves.

Yoga meditation helps calm my restless windy mind. Even students with ADHD and/or PTSD reported finding it helpful.

The last book on my course's syllabus was Tulku Thondup's *The Healing Power of Mind: Simple Meditation Exercises for Health, Well-Being, and Enlightenment* (1996), a Tibetan Buddhist approach. The book has two half-pages, under the section "Daily Living as Healing," on "Drinking and Eating." The practice is to be mindful of every taste and of the process of eating and drinking, to be aware of how it satisfies hunger and thirst and generates health in the mind and the body, and to be thankful and wish for all beings to be satisfied.

The practice reminds me of a story in the Indian epic *Mahabharata* where Krishna's hunger is satisfied by a single grain of rice, and of the practice of mindfully eating a raisin: hold it in your hand, look at it, touch it, smell it, put it in your mouth, slowly chew it, swallow it, notice how you feel afterwards.

3.

As I grow old, I feel an increasing sense of fellowship with beings who are old–elders, trees, stones, mountains, Earth. I also feel increasingly nourished by the presence of young beings, their promise of life's renewal. When I see their energy, freshness, and courage, I feel hope. At the same time, I worry about their future and the dangers to life as we know it on this planet. What are we leaving behind for the coming generations? Will humans, as a species, experience longevity, or will we be consumed by our excessive appetites and go the way of the species we have eliminated? In Buddhist terms, the windy demons of hope and fear are getting to me.

As this year moves into autumn, my balcony garden is reaching the end of its annual life cycle. Plant tissues and sinews, like my own, are becoming dry and stiff. Soon solitary bees will overwinter in them. I will move some indoor plants, but I will have to leave behind the arugula, chard, and mustard greens. I want to fabricate an on-going growing season by growing some kind of green food inside, a gesture of life going on, like the way, in the yin yang rotation, there is a seed of light in the dark and of dark in the light.

In the 1970s, when my family was young, along with canning, pickling, bread-making, and yoghurt making, I used to sprout seeds on the kitchen counter. To revive this long-ago practice, I got myself Doug Evans's *The Sprout Book: Tap into the Power of the Planet's Most Nutritious Food* (2020). Dr. Joel Fuhrman tells me, in his Foreword, "Clean green foods are the secret to a long and healthy life." The health power of green foods, he says, is most concentrated when they are young sprouts full of energy and freshness. Something to add to my longevity food lists!

I cleaned up my old Johnny's sprouting apparatus, went on Amazon to order a pound of Nature Jim's mixed salad sprouting seeds, and looked up, in *The Ayurveda Cookbook,* how to prepare sprouts, such as broccoli and mung, to avoid unbalancing *vata.* The flurry with which I rushed into this project was a typical *vata* flurry. These windy enthusiasms, usually involving on-line purchases and promises of well-being, run the risk of exhausting their energy before they get anywhere. As soon as the packages arrived, I returned them.

Meanwhile I'm reading *Buddha's Brain: The Practical Neuroscience of Happiness, Love and Wisdom* (2009) by neurologists Rick Hanson and Richard Mendius. The book shows in detail how my mental actions change my brain's activity and structure. "What flows through your mind sculpts your brain." Flurries make more flurries and more attachment to flurries.

The authors, who are contemplative practitioners, believe the mind and consciousness involve a non-physical reality, but they stick to what can be explained by science. They cannot explain the relationship between the mind's conscious experience, the brain, and the neural network pervading the body. What they can do is track the way our mental experience corresponds to the neural activity of our brain, and how the brain is in turn affected by the mind's activities and by its biological and social environment.

Science verifies why Buddhist contemplative practices calm my difficult states of mind (e.g., stress, anxiety, anger, sorrow, worry, impatience, impulsiveness). It explains how the practices cultivate positive states of mind, which generate positive changes in my brain and in my relationship with my body and with others.

Buddha's teacher, it is said, was the nature of mind knowing things as they are.

Without question then, while I'm eating my vegetables and seizing the day, as the years roll on, I plan to persevere with these practices, attend to things as they are, and monitor my flurries.

My Caterpillar Education

Having planted a garden for pollinators, I find I know nothing about them.
My teachers today are four caterpillars, bright green, black-banded with gold dots,
identified by googling as eastern black swallowtails, one smaller than the others,
getting fatter and fatter as they chew the bronze fennel on my balcony.

Wondrously the Dutchman Jan Swammerdam
biologist and curator of curiosities in the 17th century
made "little bloodless animals" his teachers with the help
of microscopes such as those with lenses by Spinoza.

He saw that, before hatching from eggs, insects form
groups of cells dormant in their larvae who,
digesting themselves in their chrysalis, fuel the cells
to divide and multiply into bodies with wings.

Chrysalis as shroud, butterfly as winged afterlife
flying from the stage of devouring to the sipping of nectar–
this progression of transport preforms in thought
like caterpillars' cell groups preform in their bodies.

Where Ovid sang of gods changing bodies to new forms,
and Lucretius sang of Nature, space, atoms, and swerves,
Swammerdam saw God's ordering Finger in a louse under microscope:
from insects to humans, all living beings develop from eggs.

A female swallowtail may lay fifty eggs a day,
one by one, pale yellow, small, for eight days,
on carrot, fennel, parsley, rue, or dill, from which larvae
(aka caterpillars) hatch within eight days. This I did not see.

I did not see the young caterpillars molt out
of their exoskeletal skin, changing again and again

as they grew over two or three weeks
to their plump mature size and bright colors.

Nor did I see how all four caterpillars disappeared overnight!
No chrysalis hangs by silk thread from nearby leaf or stem!
They are not tasty, I read. Their osmeterium emits a foul odor.
But their carotenoids give luster to a chickadee's feathers.

Their protein and fat attract sparrows, jays, titmice, and cardinals.
Of all the eggs laid, very few become butterflies. In their place I find
a tiny bee weighted down by gold pollen sacks nestling into
the last fennel flowers, just her size, atop stalks bare of leaves.

Words

1.

On Monday afternoons I go to an hour-long mindfulness meditation gathering at my local library, followed by a women's Bible study group at the local Episcopalian church. The first group, seated in a circle of folding chairs, meditates in silence for twenty minutes. Then the facilitator leads us in quiet discussion of a chapter in a contemporary Buddhist book, currently Pema Chödron's *The Wisdom of No Escape.* The Bible group is reading *Devotions for People Who Don't Do Devotions,* applying a Bible verse to an everyday life situation.

Although my spiritual practice is Buddhist and I have mixed feelings about Christianity, I value the traditional prayers, liturgies, music, and seasons of the church, their archetypal resonance that connects with other spiritual traditions, perennial psychological patterns, and a sense of community.

To help churches like ours survive when they can no longer afford their own priest, the Episcopal Diocese of New York is offering a series of lay conversations on "Learning to Lead Morning and Evening Prayer." I signed up to participate. Taught by the Canon for Congregational Vitality and Formation, the course is designed to help us understand the history and value of the *Daily Office* of structured prayer and commit more fully to its communal practice.

My mother and mother-in-law were members of a Methodist women's prayer circle. Several years ago, wanting to continue in this tradition, I started a Psalms study group in our church. It disbanded during covid and reemerged as the current women's group. Recently I tried to introduce the practice of Centering Prayer, but I lacked the skill or experience to energize that kind of spiritual instruction.

Centering Prayer was introduced in its contemporary form around fifty years ago by three Trappist monks in Massachusetts–William Meninger, Basil Pennington, and Thomas Keating. It developed from the ancient prayer method of *lectio,* reading and hearing the Word as Spirit speaks through a text of scripture.

After listening for ten minutes or so, one comes to rest in a sacred word or phrase. A contemporary simplified version is taught in retreat workshops around the world. Without first reading scripture, one asks the Spirit for guidance in choosing a suitable word. The prayer closes with a few minutes of silence. It is recommended to do this practice for at least twenty minutes twice a day. Though theologically different from Yoga and Buddhist contemplative practices, like them it involves continually returning to a simple focus for resting and quieting the mind.

On the one hand, contemporary life is high speed, noisy, provocative, not conducive to a quiet mind. On the other hand, the contemporary situation is what drives some of us to seek out methods for calming our over-stimulated minds.

Most spiritual traditions, as far as I know, include practices of personal and communal prayer. It seems that we tend to give up daily prayer to the degree we feel we have control over everything. If we pray, we may do so for some selfish end.

In the first session on leading prayer we learned that the *Daily Office* has its roots in ancient Jewish daily prayer practice. In the early church, these practices became part of Christian lay people's lives. In the sixth century, St. Benedict formalized them, and then in 1549 the Archbishop of Canterbury, Thomas Cranmer, simplified them in the first *Book of Common Prayer.* They provide a daily rhythm of morning prayer, for guidance and strength, and evening prayer, for reflection and peaceful rest, an anchor in times good and bad.

I liked the teacher's argument that structured prayer frees the spirit. It is also a model for the structure and rhythm of spontaneous prayer. It allows us to engage in prayer, with its ancient communal roots, without having to struggle with finding words.

Our modern excesses of materialism, mine among them, have uprooted us from nature and our natural inclination toward spiritual experience and practice. I feel a close relationship between the regenerative projects of botanical and spiritual rerooting. The words of the Episcopal common prayers emerged from and were transmitted through a long lineage of practitioners, just as were the prayers of my morning and evening Tibetan Buddhist practice. That practice, however, lacks a nearby venue for communal prayer as well as for gardening. At our little local church, we are hosting a Rooted Solutions project, developing a pollinator garden and removing invasives. Hopefully our next step can be saving and planting the seeds of prayer.

2.

As I progress into my second year of retirement, I am drawn to teachings and teachers less philosophical and more religious than those I explored last year. Similarly, over the course of my life, I have oscillated between a more contemplative, poetic, mystical mode and a more intellectual, rational, objective mode. It could be that the mystical mode emerges in the context of someone dying or something going wrong.

I made it a rule in retirement to include, in my readings, unread books from my over-stuffed library. To complement our conversations on the *Daily Office* I decided to take William Meninger as my Contemplative Prayer teacher via his book *The Loving Search for God* (1997), a commentary on the 14th-century anonymous Middle English spiritual classic, *The Cloud of Unknowing,* which I will also read, though not for the first time. Much as in Buddhist contemplation, it teaches a gentle way of pacifying the transient words, thoughts, images, and concepts that ordinarily course through our minds.

In Buddhism the key to this practice is *maitri,* loving kindness toward oneself and others. In *Cloud* and Christian contemplative prayer, it is love, "a loving search for God, for others, and for yourself." In both traditions, the teacher is a spiritual friend, teaching with kindness from his/ her learning and experience. Most of the 138 chapters in Meninger's book begin, "Dear friend."

Like Buddhism, Platonism, and mystical traditions, Meninger and *Cloud* distinguish between ordinary truth, known to the intellect, and ultimate truth, known beyond words and images. Verbal teachings help guide our search for truth beyond words. In the Christian tradition, this is called the *via negativa,* the path to "nothing but God." In union with God, one experiences union with everything God has made and loves.

In the non-theological Buddhist tradition, all phenomena are seen as interdependent, empty of a separate autonomous being of their own. Ultimate and ordinary truth are interdependent, relative to one another. In the meditative realization of ultimate truth, one sees that there is no difference between samsara (ordinary experience) and nirvana (ultimate realization). In our ordinary view of things, this makes no sense.

In both traditions, this ultimate insight is introduced through intellectual and verbal analysis. Then the practitioner aspires, through contemplative practice, to directly experience ultimate truth beyond words and thought. Each tradition offers a simple precise technique for redirecting the mind when it wanders. Buddhist practice focuses on the breath. *Cloud* suggests "wrapping and folding up" the contemplative intuition in a little word or syllable, such as "God" or "love." Meninger's chosen word is "Abba, Father."

The writer of *Cloud* tells us that, by "cloud," he doesn't mean darkness as in the lack of natural light. He means a "lack of knowing. Like everything you don't know or have forgotten, it is dark to you, because you do not see it with your spiritual eye....it is not called a cloud of the air, but a cloud of unknowing that is between you and your God." In contemplative practice, one puts "a cloud of forgetting" between oneself and the creaturely world. (Ch. 4-5)

Twenty-five hundred years ago, Buddha also used a cloud image in his teaching: "While the *dhammamegha* (cloud of dharma) keeps raining, may all be free from their defiling impulses." *Yogasutras* defines the "cloud of dharma" as spiritual union (samadhi).

Cloud goes on to say that "sometimes He will send out a beam of spiritual light, piercing this cloud of unknowing that is between you and Him, and show you some of His mystery, of which one may not and cannot speak." The author says he dares not speak more of that work "with my blabbering fleshly tongue." He will only speak of "that work that falls to man," the work of prayer. (Ch. 26) Similarly Buddha avoided describing his ultimate experience. He taught the practices, the path as the goal.

The author of *Cloud* quotes Denis (Pseudo-Dionysius the Areopagite, a sixth-century Syrian monk whom Medieval Christians believed was a disciple of Saint Paul): "The most goodly knowing of God is that which is knowing by unknowing." Denis' writings, he says, affirm everything in his treatise. (Ch. 70) Meninger points out that a recent Vatican document advising Christians on what is acceptable to receive or avoid from Eastern non-Christian religions recommends *Cloud* as containing the Catholic tradition on contemplative prayer. (Ch. 84) In the other Centering Prayer books I have looked at, there is concern about differentiating this practice from Eastern non-Christian practices so as to keep it clearly within the Western Christian teaching lineages.

After finishing his commentary on the *Cloud* chapters, Meninger teaches a practice he calls Compassion Meditation. (Ch. 111-118) I am familiar with this practice as Buddhist *maitri* meditation. It involves sending out loving kindness, first to a friend, then to someone about whom we have no strong feelings, and lastly to someone about whom we have strong aversion, an enemy whom we love to hate. The practice cultivates compassion and forgiveness.

Meninger's discussion of forgiveness connects to his book's concluding chapters on the Lord's Prayer. (Ch. 119-137) He points out that the disciples asked Jesus, their teacher, "Teach us how to pray." Jesus responded with a method of prayer, "an attitude from which prayers should proceed," rather than a prayer to be recited.

Chapter by chapter, Meninger considers "the meanings found in each phrase." He says that, when he began practicing discursive meditation and meditated on the Lord's Prayer, he went through the whole prayer in the twenty-minute meditation period. Then he found himself dwelling on some phrase and not going through the whole prayer. After a while he found himself meditating on just the first two words, "Our Father," or even just on the first word, "Our." Thus his discursive practice of *lectio* led him to his practice of contemplative prayer with "Father" as his chosen word.

I am inclined to choose the word "Mother," a word resonant with loving kindness and compassion in both the Buddhist and Christian traditions. Mary is the Mother of the Word. The Perfection of Wisdom is the Mother of Buddhas. In Biblical imagery, the father is associated with power, the mother with wisdom. In Buddhist imagery, the guru replaces the father.

Truth-Prints

Last night
a brief rain in hot drought
lifted the dying droops
of the buckwheat and hollyhock,
nicotiana and arugula.
A bolt flashed,
struck bone-dry woods,
travelled quickly,
burned acres and acres,
no water.

My friend
believer in holy
serendipity in old age,
waters daily
with prayer
drawn
from wells
deep below
the droughts
of the world.

My friend,
believer in holy
apocalypse in old age,
daily stores up
calamities,
digs
in his learning
like a squirrel
for nuts he left
somewhere.

"Image
is that wherein
what has been
comes together
in a flash
with the now
to form a
constellation,"
Walter Benjamin notes
in a convolute

cited
by Agamben,
The Time That Remains
(between time
and its end),
flashing
the auspicious perilous
truth-print
in a moment
of now.

Bolts flash,
strike the dried
bits I oddly stored,
energize
without words.
Morning light
mixed with shade
dapples air,
travels
toward night.

Projects

In the first issue of the *New York Review of Books* to appear after the 2024 presidential election, Zadie Smith reviewed *The Third Reich of Dreams: The Nightmare of a Nation.* The book is a translation of Charlotte Beradt's collection, first published in 1966, of ordinary German people's dreams, 1933 to 1939. In her accompanying commentary, Beradt observes how the dreamers, as they dream, react with submission and indifference to the totalitarian atmospheres of surveillance in their dreams. Smith points out how the propaganda technology and mind manipulation in the dreams and in the Third Reich are nothing compared with what we now face from the potentials of algorithms, AI, and men like Trump and Musk to suck us into "mandatory conformity" by monopolizing our attention.

Leading up to the election, those of us whose party is now in exile from political power had our attention monopolized by the blatant falsehoods, aggression, and gross behaviors of the other side, its shameless repetition of the patterns of the Third Reich, as if history had taught us nothing of catastrophe, as if tragic theater had taught us nothing about hubris, as if loss of basic moral and spiritual values is nothing to be concerned about. Alas for all the postcards I sent out urging voters to "vote for joyful warriors who protect our freedoms, families, and futures!"

Since the election I try to avoid political obsession. I busy myself locally with environmental projects and communal conversations. I meditate to keep my mind steady. I resolve to neither provoke my fears nor hide from what's to come. I have dystopian dreams. I cast humor on the situation by recalling the rebels in the Woody Allen film *Sleeper* as they fight to derail the Aries Project / Project 2025 and succeed in terminating the Leader who has been reduced to a nose.

My brother and I grew up in a household devoted to projects. Our mother gathered up old clothes to make braided rugs. In her rugs worn down in my house I can recognize clothes I once wore. Our Father crafted mostly with wood. I still have the sewing cabinet he made for my mother and the chest of drawers that went with the crib he made for me when I was born. My brother also crafts mostly with wood, though more recently also with metal. I have a cedar chest and picture frames made by him. My sister-in-law is an artist whose current projects are mosaics. She made me a beautiful mosaic of a Wisconsin birch grove. I am the only one whose projects involve words, both reading and writing them.

My brother and sister-in-law, rooted in Wisconsin, spend the wintry half of the year in New Orleans. As they get older, my brother told me yesterday, they can't leave Wisconsin until they finish their projects there because they might no longer remember what they were doing when they get back. (My brother is seventy-six.)

For a post-election reading project, I turn to teachings from Khenpo Karthar Rinpoche, my Buddhist teacher who escaped in 1959 from the Chinese takeover of Tibet, and from *The Consolation of Philosophy* by Anicius Manlius Severinus Boethius (480-524), written while he was imprisoned and awaiting execution after serving and then falling under the displeasure of the Ostrogothic king Theodoric. (The last Roman emperor was deposed in 476, completing the Empire's fall.)

While pre-Chinese Tibet, pre-Gothic Rome, pre-Nazi Germany, and pre-Trump America were all far from perfect, in each case it was a takeover hostile to long held cultural values, leaving disempowered individuals, especially writers, artists, and teachers, to keep the endangered legacies alive. Boethius's writings kept ancient philosophy alive during the Dark and early Middle Ages, including for Alan of Lille, the 12th-century poet-philosopher-theologian who was the subject of my dissertation. Tibetan teachers began opening their teachings to the west in the 1970s so that we would value them, translate them, and help them survive.

The Chinese invasion began in Eastern Tibet in 1957. In an urgent vision, a young scholar and meditation master, Khenpo Gangshar, was told to arouse his people's awareness that the Chinese can destroy their lives but not their minds. My teacher Khenpo Karthar was among those who received Gangshar's teachings. He passed them on to us during a weekend retreat in May 2013. Turning ninety at that time, he was thirty-four when he received the teachings, "The Natural Self-Liberation of Whatever You Meet," pointing out the buddha nature of the mind.

Rinpoche gave us a series of trainings, practices, and instructions for cultivating a deep non-conceptual meditative awareness that our naked mind is the root of how we experience everything. We can train to rest the mind naturally within present awareness, neither prolonging the past nor beckoning the future.

Buddhahood, Rinpoche said, is complete freedom from fixation of any kind. His distinctive presence helped us glimpse the wisdom he embodied, a wisdom hard to experience and hard to put into words. It revealed itself in his devotion to teaching, in how grateful he was to all the teachers who had kept this wisdom alive, who in their kindness had passed it on to him so he could pass it on to us. This seems to me like the ultimate human project, inseparable from compassion.

Wisdom in Sanskrit is *Prajña.* Perfect Wisdom, Prajñaparamita, is said to be the Mother of all Buddhas. Wisdom in Greek is Sophia. Philosophy is the love of wisdom. We love and seek Wisdom, Socrates said, because we do not possess it. In the Septuagint Bible, the Wisdom of Solomon is a book of Solomon's search for wisdom. He writes, "Wisdom, the fashioner of all things, taught me. There is in her a spirit that is intelligent, holy." (7:22) She is "a reflection of eternal light." (7:26) In Boethius's *Consolation,* She appears in the form of a woman standing over his head, much as Homer has Athena appear over the head of Odysseus when she comes to advise him.

Boethius was devoted to a project of transmitting Platonic and Aristotelian philosophy to his countrymen through translations and commentaries. He was also a Christian theologian who wrote five theological tractates. He presented those two schools of philosophy, theology and philosophy, and poetry and prose as complementing rather than opposed to one another.

The Consolation of Philosophy is mostly in the Platonic tradition and not conspicuously Christian. It has a hybrid interweave of poetry and prose, narrative and teaching, imagination and reason as it journeys through stages of spiritual remediation in the face of suffering and death. Its thirty-nine poems, which alternate with prose sections, contain eighteen different ancient meters in a complex system of rhythmic repetition. Traditionally read out loud, keeping the metrics alive, the poems were loved and set to music during the Middle Ages.

Before Boethius's imprisonment, when Lady Philosophy used to appear in his well-appointed library, he learned about the classic Platonic contemplative ascent from sensory to intellectual things, from unreliable opinion to sure knowledge. In despair in his prison cell, bereft of his books, he pictures Philosophy chiding him for having forgotten what he once knew about the unreliability of Fortune, a fickle goddess who "takes a pleasure in turning things upside down." (II.2.30)

Philosophy misses her seat of honor in his mind, not in his library. (I.5.23) His mind is occupied with the shadows of things, with lost wealth, honor, power, glory, and pleasure. "Have you no proper and inward good, that you seek your goods in those things which are outward and separated from you?" (II.5.70)

Her argument is compelling, he says, but the chief cause of his sorrow remains. If we believe that the governor of all things is good, how is there any evil at all, and moreover how does it go unpunished, while virtue is punished? This is the great question.

Beatitude, She tells him, is the very goodness for which all things are done. Insofar as a person lacks goodness in their actions, that lack is their punishment. They become, degree by degree, less human—in greed like a wolf, in deceit like a fox, in rage like a lion, in fear like a deer, in laziness like an ass, in lust like a sow. (IV.3.9-10)

Since justice is good, bad actors lack that good and acquire further evil if they are not justly punished. (IV.4.70) "In wise men, there is no place for hatred... Vice is a sickness of mind...rather worthy of compassion than of hatred." (IV.4.149-154) She sums this up at the end of a poem: "Love then the good, and pity thou the ill." (IV.m4.12)

His philosophical/theological questions, She tells him, "though useful to understand, carry us off the journey we've begun." (V.1.10) That journey was to recover "the beauty of his mind." (I.m2.24)

At the end of Her last poem, She gives him practical advice for his recovery. "Don't let thoughts weigh down your mind. Don't let your mind be oppressed by your body." (V.m5.13-15) Her final advice, in the following prose section, is to shun vices, cultivate virtues, let hope raise your spirit, and offer humble prayers. (V.6.173-176)

Reading Boethius still feels to me like an impersonal doctoral exercise. Meanwhile the outrages of this administration are proceeding from bad to worse, its Project 2025 in full swing. As it wrecks vengeance on those it regards with displeasure, Boethius's situation becomes less remote. It could happen here and now.

2.

I live in a wooded townhouse community. Across from my house, new neighbors have cut down eleven beautiful old trees. It feels like a hostile takeover of my neighborhood.

Even more than my initial rage, I feel grief, a sense of mourning and sorrow over the loss of the nearby trees, particularly the tall white pine and radiant red maple I used to contemplate from my front windows. The years of the cut trees' history are recorded, ring by ring, from long before I was born, in their stumps, their grave-markers, memorials I visit every day. Their cutting was for me a last straw in the global accumulation of actual and potential environmental trespasses and denials, including by those whom the 2024 election has empowered. I have been on edge for a long time.

I have taught and attended environmental courses extolling the value of trees. Some of the courses I taught, such as Indigenous Spirituality and Environmental Activism, included learning from Indigenous people's traditional relationship with nature. We explored how trees and groves are sacred in ancient and current nature-based cultures. We read stories of people, mostly women, over the course of history, sacrificing their lives for trees.

Among their many virtues, trees support pollinators, sequester carbon and release oxygen, prevent soil erosion, stabilize the water cycle, improve air quality, and provide shade and beauty. My town and my townhouse community are committed to the preservation and planting of trees, which is one reason I moved here.

I read in David Pogue's book, *How to Prepare for Climate Change: A Practical Guide to Surviving the Chaos* (2021), of a new mental health field, ecotherapy, for treating grief, depression, and panic as sane and valid responses to our current environmental crises. He points out that we experience, along with polarized social conflict, inner psychological conflict, since our modern lifestyle is responsible for our environmental problems. Our cultural identity feels threatened. We have not been able to sufficiently reverse course. Now we have to live with the consequences. (Next Thursday Pogue is giving a pep talk in my privileged upscale area to help us prepare for catastrophe.)

The new neighbors see every tree on their property as about to fall on their house. They see trees' roots as a danger to their house's foundations. Looking at their property, we have entirely different views and emotions. In my townhouse community, new residents no longer want to post and share their contact information with other residents. They prefer privacy. I guess everyone is trying to survive in their own way.

Pogue recommends action as the antidote to our climate despair and feelings of impotence. He gives instructions for mitigating our carbon footprint, links for ways to exert political pressure, and a list of ways to relieve stress, including exercise, enjoying nature, taking time off from the news and from worrying, and engaging in creative arts.

I do most of these things and resolve to do more. I put up a seed tube and suet feeder among the trees in my very small patio area. My old neighbor always had lots of birds around the feeders among the trees in his backyard. The new neighbors have cut these trees to stumps. The feeders are gone.

I remember having emotions about trees when I was very young. My first memory was of watching the light and shadow of a mountain ash tree play as I lay in my cradle. When I was around seven, for some reason the big pine tree at the corner of our front yard was cut down. I loved to sit under that tree. I remember sitting there and crying when my mother cut my braids off. The tree was my teacher of calm. It sequestered my tears.

Every year during harvest season we drove from Milwaukee, Wisconsin, to Fredonia, New York, to my grandpa's farm with its orchards and vineyards. We came back with a trunk full of several kinds of grapes, pears, and apples. Over the years, the trip changed from country roads to bigger and bigger highways. I had nightmares of riding in a kind of tractor with a long blade to the side, severing all the trees and plants along the road and replacing them with endless shelves of things for sale, turning landscape into supermarket.

I used to spend summers at a Girl Scout camp in the Wisconsin Northwoods. Now I walk every day in the grounding and uplifting society of trees. As in my first memory, or perhaps projecting that memory back from now, I feel mystery and beauty in their shadows' play with light, their holy breath, their dance and their quiet.

India's ashrams, centers of learning and peace, were traditionally in a forest. Sitting under a tree, Buddha achieved enlightenment. My forebears emigrated from the German Black Forest. I have spent most of my life in the Algonquin regions of the Northeastern American woods, in the contemplative groves of OM, and in the dialogic groves of academe, descendants of Plato's school in its olive grove outside of city walls, outside the centers of power, gathering words of wisdom like acorns and hazelnuts.

March Moon / *Onaabani-Giizis*

Deep crusted snow mirrors
the white glow of the Hard
Crust on the Snow Moon

except on the iced lake
where snow soft and deep
thaws into its own lake.

Unseen in the frozen world
bears nurse their babies,
coyotes mate, ravens nest,

wolves prepare to be born,
maple sap rises, while we humans
are about to save daylight.

As for me, I will honor
National Napping Day, today
on the Ojibway calendar.

History and the Moon

When I was in seventh grade, assigned to write an autobiography, I gave it the title *Luna or the Phases of the Moon.* I don't remember what I wrote about myself or how it related to the moon. I do remember, for most of my life until I turned sixty, feeling mood phases of depletion and fullness, ebb and flow, sometimes pushing toward extremes at each end. Even now, although well past my reproductive years, I wear a pearl ring prescribed by an ayurvedic astrologer to stabilize my moon and a sapphire ring to stabilize my Saturn which, he said, decreased its dark shadow over me when I turned sixty. More significantly, at sixty I had begun to practice Buddhist meditation. In the classic Buddhist picture of the Wheel of Life, the Buddha points to the full moon as a symbol of dharma, of tranquil mind seeing things as they are, beholding life's wheel and our wandering with equanimity and compassion.

During my moodier years I gravitated toward German romanticism. In the Schubert/Seidl song "The Wanderer to the Moon," the unsettled poet contrasts himself with the moon, at home wherever it is. In "To the Moon," Goethe contemplates what "wanders by night through the heart's labyrinth." Wanderers gazing at the moon are on display in a current Caspar David Friedrich show at the Metropolitan Museum. They remind me how, growing up, I used to watch the moon rising over the depths of Lake Michigan, its farther shore unseen, a stimulant to my wanderlust.

Through the practice of meditation, I have become less of a wanderer. Impacted by old age, thrift, carbon footprint concerns, and a sense of world disorder, my journeying has turned local and inward. During meditation, thoughts come and go. Autobiography, history, and time fade into abstractions. Still, Hermetic moon wanderings and cycling constellations of feelings, images, language, and thought continue to engage my mind.

My favorite novels are novels of education, especially those by George Eliot and Thomas Mann. I recently embarked on a project of reading Mann's tetralogy *Joseph and His Brothers.* I can see from the inscription that my husband gave me this book in 1986, "as a model," he wrote, when I was undertaking to write a historical novel of ideas, a trilogy about the Great Moguls Akbar, Jahangir, and Shah Jahan and their wives. I was so immersed in India at the time that I left it to my husband to read the tetralogy. Only now, almost forty years later, have I become ready to journey into this culmination of Mann's linguistic, mythological, and psychological complexity and irony, however much, on this first reading, will pass me by.

It is mid-March 2025. Trump's second presidency so far, with its Blitzkrieg of disturbances, its constant endangerment of civilized norms, has been, like Nazi rule, a hostile takeover certified by a democratic election. As in Emperor worship, only those who join the Trump cult are safe from his ire.

Mann wrote *Joseph and His Brothers* from 1926 to 1943, the fourth part in California during his exile from Nazi Germany. The lengthy project became his source of stability and comfort, his rod and his staff, he said, as he walked through the valley of the shadow of death. It was his favorite among his writings, and now it is becoming mine.

My 1983 one-volume English translation by H. T. Lowe-Porter is 1207 pages long. I am reading a three-volume German edition, and thus far have only completed the first volume. Although Mann explicitly identifies as a modern secular person, his/the narrator's voice is intriguingly archaic, like a cultural practitioner committed to keeping alive linguistic, mythic, and spiritual traces of the past (spiritual in the non-theological German sense of *Geistlich,* involving morality, beauty, truth). Its complexity, both in German and in the translation, is of a piece with Joseph's educated way of thinking and talking, in contrast with the rude macho boorishness of Joseph's brothers.

Addressing his readers in the middle of the 20th century, Mann/the narrator voices his striving to know the meaning of "our own normally unsatisfied and quite abnormally wretched existences." Finding the well of the past, "of the earliest formations of humanity," unfathomable, he comes to rest, "personally and historically," in a point of time forming a particular "communion of faith," the one inherited by young Joseph, the one in which Joseph's mentor Eliezer has been educating him. (p. 3)

The story Joseph has inherited begins with Abraham, whom the narrator describes as "a brooding and inwardly unquiet man," a man who wandered and roved "as the moon did...because he found it most right and fitting to his unsatisfied, doubting, yes, tormented state." (p. 4) In the classic theology of Paul and Luther, what distinguishes Abraham is that his "faith counted as righteousness." Taking a more existential approach, Mann focuses on Abraham's doubt, questioning, and unsettlement. Mann also pictures Joseph as aware that, although he sometimes thinks of Abraham as his great-grandfather, twenty generations in his era's chronology, around six hundred Babylonian years, separate him from this beginning of his inherited story. Joseph thinks of both timings as true, of dualities as exchangeable.

As the narrator wanders on, we learn that young Joseph has "certain tender and spiritual affiliations with the moon." (p. 15) The art of writing and its patron Thoth are both associated with the moon, and Joseph, unlike his brothers, is literate. He recognizes himself as less restless than his father Jacob, more into "pomp and world circumstance." He knows that the spirit forbade Jacob, a herdsman, to settle in towns, for Jacob "served a God whose nature was not repose and abiding comfort, but a God of designs for the future, in whose will inscrutable, great, far-reaching things were in process of becoming, who, with His brooding will and His world-planning, was Himself only in process of becoming, and thus was a God of unrest, a God of cares, who must be sought for, for whom one must at all times keep oneself free, mobile and in readiness." (p. 31) This too is Joseph's spiritual inheritance.

Mann/the narrator goes on to identify, as a story-teller, with this inheritance. "I will not conceal my own native and comprehensive understanding of the old man's restless unease and dislike of any fixed habitation....To me too has not unrest been ordained, have not I too been endowed with a heart which knoweth not repose? The story-teller's star—is it not the moon, lord of the road, the wanderer, who moves in his stations, one after another, freeing himself from each? For the story-teller makes many a station, roving and relating, but pauses only tent-wise, awaiting further directions..." (p. 32)

While the story-teller makes his stations in linear historical sequence, he carries old baggage in his caravan. Personalities, relationships, situations, themes, etc. reappear, generating cycles of archetypal recurrence. The drama builds through these rhythms, tempos, and counterpoints. Joseph's complex psychology and cultural history intone as inner voices in polyphonic layers. His thoughts when his brothers leave him to die in the well are "like a moving music, perpendicularly composed, which his spirit was occupied in conducting." (p. 384) In this way Mann transposes layers of the sub-conscious and archeology harmonically. (Mann mentions Wagner's *Ring* cycle as a musical inspiration for shaping the book as a tetralogy.)

Mythology and Humanism: The Correspondence of Thomas Mann and Karl Kerenyi (1975) casts some light for me on Mann's thoughts about his approach to the story. In a 1936 letter, he wrote that he found appealing "the secularization of the concept of religion, its psychological conversion into the profane spheres of morality and the soul. Religion as the opposite of negligence and disregard, as taking care, respecting, considering, conscience, as a *vigilant* attitude...a concerned, attentive receptivity to the movements of the universal spirit." This corresponds with young Joseph having to learn he had failed to consider that everything is not about him, with no regard for his brothers.

In a 1941 letter Mann reflected that he was drawn to Hermes as lord of the way. Like Thoth, Hermes is the moon-oriented patron of narrators, learning, wisdom, and writing. He is an intermediary, translator, and wanderer. I too am drawn to him. He is Joseph's and therefore Mann's—or Mann's and therefore Joseph's—patron in this project, guiding them both as they mediate between Abrahamic revelation and Ancient Near Eastern polytheistic cultures, and guiding Mann's mediation between the Biblical world and modern German and western culture.

In his 1948 Foreword about seeing the first one-volume English edition, Mann reflects on the novel's polyphony, its "pleasure in changing its linguistic masks as often as its hero changes his God-masks." In the final novel, written in California, Joseph becomes "an American Hermes" and the narrator's German becomes Americanized, shedding some of its previous archaic flavors. Mann refers to the whole, rather mischievously, as "a humorous song of mankind." It ends with Joseph caring for his brothers after they have betrayed him. He bears them no animosity. Their history, he tells them, is God's play.

I find it interesting that Mann's interpretation of the relationship between the story's deep past and his/the narrator's present time was influenced by J.J. Bachofen's book *Mother Right* (1861). Bachofen had influenced me forty years ago when I was immersed in the myths of Indian goddesses. A Swiss jurist and historian of Roman law, he critiqued modern civilization as a patriarchal solar culture suppressing older nomadic and agrarian nature-oriented maternal lunar cultures. Roman civil law, he argued, established the masculine rule that came to dominate western civilization, with its drive toward rational imperial control of all life and the whole world, and its elimination of matricentric traditions.

Drawing from Bachofen, Mann wrote, in his "Schopenhauer" essay, about the moon as the intermediary between the solar and the earthly, the spiritual and the material, the immortal and the mortal, the male and female worlds. It is the purest of earthly bodies and the impurest of heavenly bodies. It is androgynous, Lunus and Luna, feminine in relation to the sun and masculine in relation to the earth. In this way, Bachofen says, the moon "maintains the unity of the cosmos, it is the interpreter between mortals and immortals." "This mediation," Mann writes, "is the source of their irony." By "their" he means the dualities.

Mann's ironic humor is especially manifest in the androgynous, lovely and vain, charming and insensitive, intelligent and contriving, wise and foolish personality of young Joseph. Much of the story revolves around the way Joseph enchants some people and provokes others. He identifies and is identified with his late mother Rachel, Jacob's beloved, and also with the Sumerian mythical figure of Dumuzi, an archetypal dying-and-rising god. He is particularly known for his dreams and his interpretation of dreams. Mann pictures him as mediating between the symbols, myths, and legends of the Egyptian, Sumerian, and Canaanite cultures of his time, as well as of his forebears.

Bachofen wrote that ancient peoples' symbols aim inward, whereas rational language aims outward. Deriving from the centers of dream, not of waking consciousness, symbols communicate "the sublimely beautiful ideas of the past to an age that is very much in need of regeneration." Clearly Mann finds his mythic immersion personally regenerative. It enabled him to move back and forth between this project and giving public lectures, actively engaging with the historical turmoil of his times. Now in my time of historical turmoil, I find myself regenerated by Mann's immersion.

As he concludes the Prelude, "Descent into Hell," Mann/the narrator reflects on the story's descent into the past as a tasting of "death and knowledge" causing him both "eagerness" and "fear and pallor." (p. 33) The story, he says, will venture into a far deeper past than the past he has been accustomed to visit. It is "the dead-and-gone world, to which my own life shall more and more profoundly belong....To die: that means actually to lose sight of time, to travel beyond it, to exchange for it eternity and presentness and therewith for the first time, life. For the essence of life is presentness." (p. 32) This knowledge, he says, can only be gained through the initiatory experience of death. Myths and their related rituals convey intimations of its mystery to the uninitiated.

Mann was sixty-eight, with twelve years yet to live, when he reached the end of his Joseph story. One of my thoughts when I began this reading project was that, at eighty-three, I could not be certain that I would finish it, nor could I be certain that I will live to see a less disturbing historical present than the one we face today. Mann's sustaining insight that "the essence of life is presentness" is an insight for which I also train in Buddhist meditation practice.

Yesterday I read the part of *Young Joseph* where Joseph's brothers' long-brewing hatred of him explodes into a brutal attack. They beat him, strip him of the gorgeous robe that symbolizes his usurpation of primacy with their father, tie him up, throw him in a dry well, and cover the well with a cracked stone. Joseph, a good-looking, articulate, educated, wily seventeen-year-old admired by everyone but his brothers, had never imagined anyone would not love him.

Given the Nazi context in which Mann wrote the tetralogy, I can't help but feel, in his portrayal of Joseph, the illusions of Weimar culturati and, in my present MAGA context, the illusions I share with American and global liberals in the educated professional class now under siege. Like Joseph, despite all our knowledge, we are clueless about our brothers' aggressive hostility.

Mann/the narrator writes that he will hold back from describing the worst brutalities the brothers committed. Although he describes them as behaving and sounding like animals, he says he does not want readers to entirely exclude them from the realm of humanity. He describes their inner conflicts and sufferings. The nature of humans, what I think of as our collective karma, is his stated topic.

Having been thrown into the well, Joseph, always adroit with words, cries out to his brothers with a penitential cry echoing Psalm 130, *De profundis,* reechoed in Luther's hymn and Bach's cantata "Out of the depths." Hearing their plan to bloody the torn robe and tell their father an animal killed him, his concern for his father's grief juxtaposes with the brothers' desire for their father's love, which they hope to have once Joseph is not there to monopolize it. On a subtler level, they are haunted by their hands' memory of the tenderness of his body and skin as they carried him to the well. They finally move away from the well to avoid hearing Joseph's cries and feeling his presence. They cover the well with its circular stone cover cracked into two parts. Like the new moon before it is reborn, he is in the dark below for three days.

Daylight and moonlight cycle down to him through the crack between the two parts of the stone. As his consciousness slips away, the narrator tells us that "the great certainty guiding his life was belief in the unity of the dual in the fact of the revolving sphere, the exchangeability of above and below, one turning into the other," just as the light of sun, moon, and stars dies and reappears. "And therein Joseph's hope that he might live justified itself by faith." (pp. 299 & 301)

As I write this, it is the penitential season of Lent. It is also the approach of the thirty-third anniversary of my husband's death, my personal Orphic season, raising up memories from the shadow world where they dimly abide. For several years after my husband died, I immersed myself in Christ's story and the pre-Christian death and rebirth fertility myths of Osiris, Baal, Dumuzi, and Dionysius and their goddess counterparts. I had previously immersed myself in these mythopoetic and psychological archetypes, along with those of Shiva and Devi, when my parents and sister-in-law died a little more than ten years before.

For the last twenty or so years I have focused on cultivating an ethical and psychological realism that is quite the opposite of myth. Still, I feel truth in these old myths and mysteries, in their dreamlike trust in the cycles of life and death. They are a playful narrative counterpart to the Buddhist view of sacred world and the interconnection of all phenomena. In Mann's novel, their deep rhythms carry me along like tides under a swelling moon.

Little Spirit Moon

when the moon waxed to full

the whiteness of her light nourished the night

like a cup of warm milk

or the bowl of rice porridge given Buddha by a girl

when he after fasting sat under a tree

in quest of a way in the middle

between too much and too little

a way imaged by the moon its light

ungrasped by death's lord holding

life's wheel

The Horizontal and the Vertical

During my initial visit to the Metropolitan Museum's Caspar David Friedrich exhibit "The Soul of Nature" I was unpleasantly jarred by his works that feature sky-piercing crosses, often on mountain peaks. I felt drawn to his more nuanced horizontal landscapes, especially "Monk by the Sea," "Evening," and "Moonrise by the Sea." This was partly, I think, because my reading of Robert Rosenblum's book *Modern Painting and the Northern Romantic Tradition: Friedrich to Rothko* (1975) had led me to enjoy Rothko's abstract modernizations of Friedrich's uncluttered horizons and, post 1975, Agnes Martin's abstract horizontal line paintings.

Infrared photography has revealed that Friedrich painted over the vertical presence of two sail boats so that only the small figure of the monk juxtaposes the horizontal in "Monk by the Sea." In contrast, in "The Wanderer above a Sea of Mist," the poster painting for this exhibit, the vertical thrust of a dominant human figure atop a rocky mountain peak blocks our view of the misted depths he beholds. Like the crosses, that painting jarred me unpleasantly on this viewing, whereas it had not done so in the past.

On rereading Rosenblum's book, I found myself intrigued by his discussion of Barnett Newman, whom I had previously overlooked. Newman's trademark is vertical "zips" in a field of color "without atmosphere," an abstract parallel to Friedrich's crosses and solitary wanderer. The zips also made me think of the refrain from "Anthem," my favorite Leonard Cohen song: "Ring the bells that still can ring. Forget your perfect offering. There is a crack in everything. That's how the light gets in."

In his essay "The Sublime Is Now" (1948), Newman similarly argues against "the absolutisms of perfect creations" and "the postulate of beauty as an ideal." We confuse these, he says, with our natural artistic desire to express our relation to the Absolute. By the Absolute he means our absolute emotions, particularly our "urge to be exalted," to ring bells. The American abstract painter, he says, concerns himself "with the reality of the transcendental experience," not, like the European painter, with known images as transcendent objects.

Newman was painting, in the aftermath of World War II, with a sense of human moral crisis amplified by the great depression, two world wars, and the atomic bomb. I am thinking of this now as the liberal world order, established eighty years ago in that aftermath, is unravelling, and as our human impact on the natural world order causes chaotic weather, species loss, collapsing glaciers, extraction-gutted landscapes, polluted waters, and denial of this crisis and generation of fake emergencies by the current U.S. administration. My aversion to Friedrich's crosses may be in part an offshoot of my aversion to the empowered party's commitment to politicized Christian conservatism. Whereas Friedrich, I learn, painted lofty crosses in symbolic counter-statement to Napoleon's occupation of his homeland, I had seen them as Christian right-wing occupations of nature and my country. Also as a political symbol, Friedrich painted the Wanderer in an old-German costume worn by liberals during the Wars of Liberation and forbidden under the repressive regime that followed, whereas I saw the climber's seeming arrogance. I became curious to learn more about Newman's exalting vertical.

Newman was an erudite student of philosophy, biology, ornithology, and geology and a politically engaged liberal. Like Leonard Cohen, his family spirituality was in the Jewish tradition, and he was also interested in Indigenous and other mystical traditions. He made his breakthrough zip painting, the first painting he said felt truly like him, rendering a feeling of his own totality, separateness, and individuality, on his birthday, January 29, 1948. He named it "Onement I" and stopped painting for almost a year to live with it, to process what it was communicating to him.

I may have developed my horizontal preference because of my Buddhist orientation, reckoning not so much with individuality as with the interdependence and impermanence of all phenomena, the flow of the mindstream and karmic winds desolidifying notions of self. In contrast, Newman has said, "The self, terrible and constant, is for me the subject matter of painting."

For Newman, versed in Jewish mysticism, the title "Onement" suggests At-Onement, Atonement, Yom Kippur's atoning process of rebirth and renewal, the mystery of re-creation. In the *Zohar* [lit. "Brightness"] Newman would have read, "It is only when he is complete that a man is called 'one.'" In a kabbalistic commentary on Isaac Luria he would have read of the primordial man and the divine light. "The first being which emanates from...the fullness of divine light was...Adam Kadman, the primordial man. Adam Kadman is nothing but a first configuration of the divine light which flows from the essence of the Hidden God into the primeval space of the Tzim-Tzum [the vacuum essential to the true act of creativity]–not indeed from all sides, but like a beam, in one direction only."

Through the physical, mental, and emotional act of painting Onement, Newman had glimpsed a mystery of human meaning and wholeness. That direct experience, that recurring individual creation out of chaos, he said, is the subject of his paintings. He speaks of the zip as a flash of light illuminating a wholeness. He wants viewers to stand close to his paintings, in immediate contact, as in person-to-person contact.

He evokes in his art a sense of sacred place as in a synagogue, where "each man can be called up to stand before the Torah to read his portion...under the tension of that 'Tzim-Tzum' that created light and the world, he can experience a total sense of his own personality before the Torah and His Name." The artist's concern, he said, speaking of himself, is "not with his own feelings or with the mystery of his own personality but with the penetration into the world mystery....To that extent his art is concerned with the sublime. It is a religious art which through symbols will catch the basic truth of life."

Newman wrote a lot and was given to pithy quotable sayings. About humans he said, "modern man, living in times of the greatest terror the world has known...is his own terror." About the arts he said, "What is the explanation of the seemingly insane drive of man to be painter and poet if it is not an act of defiance against man's fall and an assertion that he return to the Garden of Eden? For artists are the first men."

He curated, promoted, and wrote about exhibitions of what he non-pejoratively called "primitive art," meaning Indigenous art. Whereas abstraction was considered an elite modern movement, he pointed out Indigenous artists' use of abstract shapes as "a vehicle for an abstract thought-complex, a carrier of awesome feelings felt before the terror of the unknowable." He identified with the artists' "ritualistic will toward metaphysical understanding" and "urge to be exalted."

He was an inspiring spokesperson for the personal and social value of art and was ambivalent about the relation of art to money. In one of his articles responding to an exhibition of pre-Columbian stone sculpture, he wrote: "In art, the tangible expression of man's innermost, intangible, spiritual aspirations, we have a great school for interhuman learning. Through art, we comprehend the deep stirrings of man's soul. Friendship based on the comprehension of each other's art will be founded, therefore, on a common moral purpose and will do a great deal to accomplish the world unity we all desire, since it is by comprehending the spiritual aspirations of human beings that permanent bonds can best be built." I say Amen to that!

I went to the Museum of Modern Art to view his first very wide (eighteen feet wide) painting, "Vir Heroicus Sublimis" (1950/1951). (Although "Onement I" is owned by MoMA, it is not currently in view.) Within those eighteen feet there are five narrow zips of varying color and asymmetrical placement. The painting has intense presence and mystery. I stood close beside it and found it strangely joyous and uplifting. Newman has said, "Life, as is a true work of art, is, after all, always positive." The five zips each speak their individual truth while sensing their relationship of place and tone within the whole.

In an interview two months before his death in 1970, Newman said, "I still believe that my work, in terms of its social impact, does denote the possibility of an open society, of an open world, not of a closed institutional world." His words are as inspiring now as they were in his time, perhaps moreso.

I would like to see his "Stations of the Cross, Lama Sabachthani ('Why have you forsaken me?')" series (1958-1966) at the National Gallery of Art. I am looking instead at the archive.org digitized catalogue for the 1966 initial exhibit of the Stations at the Guggenheim. Its verticals, black, white, or grey on creamy raw canvas, range from very narrow to very wide and solid to modulated, painted variously with oil paint and three different synthetic media. To the fourteen Stations he adds a fifteenth painting entitled "Be II," in the place of Resurrection. This one has a slightly modulated narrow red zip on the left and a solid narrow black zip on the right.

"Why is," Newman writes, "the question that has no answer...the original question...the unanswerable question of human suffering, an expression of each man's agony." Although he did not begin with the idea of a series on the Stations, his recovery from a heart attack in 1958 and his brother's death in 1961 were experiences provoking the theme of the human cry. His affirmation of life, self, and art asks the unanswerable question.

Lawrence Alloway, in his introductory essay for the Guggenheim catalogue, points out how Newman retained a tradition of heroic gesture and style in the act of the artist rather than in the depiction of an embodied hero. His titles evoke and pay homage to a non-idolized heroic presence, thus democratizing the heroic act.

Alloway also points out how Newman's Stations developed "through a process of self-recognition," one by one, over a period of eight years. Classically, as in the Delphic saying, "know thyself," our first self-recognition is of our mortality, the via dolorosa. The second is of the mystery beyond death, beyond the last Station.

As I page through the sequence of Stations, I pretend I am walking from one to another in their gallery in Washington. My movement is horizontal. The zips' beams and shadows orient me vertically. I think of Exodus, the people being led out of Egypt and through the wilderness with a pillar of cloud by day and a pillar of fire by night.

Crane Watch on Madeline Island

Humans set this boardwalk over boreal bog
lest we trample fragrant carpets, wintergreen, blueberry,
shrub juniper, lichen, and moss, red and white pine roots,
sponge of sand and peat on a fragile spit
between wave-washed beach and a quiet lagoon.
Surf and wind silence the sound of my footsteps.

Nearby, blended amidst patterns of pine shadows,
two slender gray forms ruffle their feathers,
spread wings, tilt and turn, jump and glide,
pivot, then stroll out from the bog's shade
for a walk on the beach, their undulant shapes
merging now with blown beach grass.

Eyes searching for things I can't see, I move on
and almost fail to see, next to the boardwalk,
a baby hawk, maybe five inches high,
motionless, soundless, wide-eyed,
seated on the ground amidst moss and lichen,
nestless beneath a leafless tree.

The Shape of My Shadow

1.

We were told to gaze at our shadow on the ground, focusing on the throat, for ten minutes, then look up.

I saw a huge man form, naked and male as I was not, projected on the sky.

I was perplexed that its shape was not the shape of my shadow, which wore a long skirt and had the contours of a woman.

Our teacher was a *Svetambara* (white-clad) Jain yogi. Another order of Jain yogis is *Digambara* (sky-clad, naked).

As a symbol of his commitment to non-violence, he wore a small white cloth over his mouth.

He taught us to chant OM and other mantras to purify our karma, remove our mental conflicts, protect ourselves and heal others.

We learned to treat illnesses with colors and seed sounds channeled through our fingers.

He had a healing effect on me, though I was not able to heal others.

He taught that souls evolve from mineral to plant to animal to human. In our human embodiments, we are still attached to our animal past, prone to violence and conflict.

Negative karma from harmful acts over countless lifetimes accrues to our souls.

Purified, the soul shines like a diamond or a star, bright and clear.

In statues, usually of gleaming white marble, Jain masters are depicted naked with a jewel at the heart center.

In Sravanabelagola in South India there is an 18-meter monolithic statue of a sky-clad Jain master, Lord Gomateshwara.

The ancient Greeks called the sky-clad Jains *gymnosophists,* naked philosophers.

It has been more than fifty years since I was perplexed by the man form projected on the sky. I never saw it again, except in my mind.

What I saw was like a sky version of the giant men in the effigy burial mounds of Wisconsin, my home state.

Some of these have been ploughed over and appear only as soil shadows.

The Man Mound near my brother's house is huge, 218 feet long, viewed from a high platform. Before he was known to be there, his legs got cut off by a highway.

Elsewhere, along with man effigies, there are birds, bear, beaver, buffalo, dogs, deer, panthers, turtles, and unidentifiables.

Late Woodland people built these mounds, it is believed, to balance and renew the world. People gathered around them in ceremony, healing rituals, and the telling of stories.

They sought a balance of the lower earth-water world and the upper air-sky world. Bears and long-tailed forms are considered earth-water spirits. Birds, birdmen, and humans are air-sky spirits.

The people's social clans may also have divided into "those above" and "those on earth."

It may be that giant human effigies were related to the War-People or Hawk clans. Most of them wear horns. They may depict a shaman or a warrior hero named Red Horn. Stories tell of his battles with giants, his death, and his rebirth.

The dead were buried in the head and/or heart of the effigy.

Sometimes, along with or instead of human bodies, burned and blackened rocks and stones were ritually arranged along with colored soils, charcoal, and ash from ceremonies that renew earth.

Burials had their appointed times. Corpses were put in temporary resting places to await the proper times.

The mounds follow the contours of the land. Bird-spirit mounds are on high ground, water-spirit mounds close to water, bear-spirit mounds in between.

With the shift to agriculture and permanent villages around 800 years ago, burials were done in cemeteries with individual graves, ceremonies focused on fertility, and the mounds were overgrown and forgotten.

Colonization outlawed Indigenous spiritual practices and languages.

It was almost forgotten that, when Grandmother Sky Woman gave birth to humans, she gave them a soul-spirit that could dream, receive visions, and see the light auras of bodies.

Their soul-spirits can return to Earth as watchers guarding the northern woodlands where they lived, including in the Hudson Valley where I live now.

I learned about this in a local Algonquin Culture workshop called "Connecting with the Landkeepers."

I picture them, transparent as shadow or wind, walking among the trees behind my house, pentimenti in the denaturalized canvas of exurbia.

2.

After my Jain teacher died, I began going to Buddhist teachers.

Buddhists picture negative karma like wind blowing the mindstream.

Buddha requested that he not be depicted in bodily form after he died. He had purified all karmic taints, was "thus gone" from his body, and would not be reborn.

He was commemorated in stupas, heaped earth mounds with the appearance of upside-down bowls.

Sculptors depicted his empty sandals and meditation cushion.

Some centuries later artists began to make Buddha forms with thirty-two emblem marks to convey his on-going compassion.

The contemporary Chinese sculptor Zhang Huan makes Buddha forms from compressed incense ash he collects from Buddhist temples in and around Shanghai.

His three-legged Buddha is a twelve ton, twenty-eight feet tall metal incense burner with three dancing legs emerging from the top of a cast of Zhang Huan's head which is partly buried in the ground on a hill in Storm King Art Center near where I live.

The legs are modeled on fragments from Buddha statues he saw destroyed in Chinese Tibet.

His Sydney Buddha is a five-meter sculpture of ash with aluminum support.

He has said that it "conveys the collective memory, soul, thoughts, prayers, and collapse of mankind."

He has written the Heart Sutra on his naked body: *emptiness is form, form is emptiness.*

In another naked performance he covered his body with honey and sat in a fly-filled public latrine in Beijing where he became covered with flies.

In his "Peace No. 2" sculpture, a bell is inscribed with his family members' names and his assistants' dreams, and a gold-leafed bronze nude cast of himself dangles in mid-air, his head as the bell clapper.

The bell symbolizes the wisdom of emptiness. Zhang Huan's head as the clapper symbolizes the jewel of compassion.

Following my teachers' instructions, I visualize the wisdom of emptiness (of how all things are interdependent and none exist entirely on their own) as the Great Mother, Prajñaparamita, Perfection of Wisdom, the body of truth, the mother of all buddhas.

She is pictured golden in color, wrapped in jeweled ornaments and diaphanous cloths. Of her four arms, the lower two are in meditation, the upper left holds a book, the right holds a thunderbolt, image of compassion.

Her book contains the Heart Sutra and the shortest wisdom sutra, the syllable AH. It reminds me of my dreams where my grandmother hands me a book.

My Life as a Solitary Bee

Today, to the brassy call of trumpets
sounding in sunbeams
and the gold libations of tree pollens,
the solitary bees, awakened
from winter sleep in stems and tubes,
busy themselves stretching their wings
and fluffing their body furs in the dazzled air.
Under last year's brittle stalks
new sprouts have barely poked their noses
or broken through the crusty ground.
Then, as the sunbeams tuck their brass
into a case of clouds and the pollens' dust
settles in shadow, the bees,
easily excited and easily dormant,
return to their solitude
as I do to my study.

Keeping and Losing Track of Time

1.

When cancer was taking over my father's body and he was bedridden for the last few weeks of his life, he kept his day-date watch on. He was an engineer and builder habituated to measurement.

Although he was an impressively large man—six feet five inches tall, two hundred eighty-five pounds—he had been losing pounds rapidly and his watchband hung slack on his wrist. The day we heard of his diagnosis, a great tree fell in our front yard. Now he lay at home in the borrowed hospital bed like a fallen tree. He was sixty-seven. He said, "I'm done for."

I think his watch reassured him that all things have their measure. He could trust that life and time, with its minutes, hours, days, and years, would go on without him.

He had begun his career as a hydraulic engineer, working on projects involving flood control and dams, and eventually on the Saint Lawrence seaway project which would open the Great Lakes to ocean-going vessels and, among other things, challenge the ecology of waters sacred to Indigenous Americans among whom, eighteen years after his death, he would begin to have descendants. He left that project in its planning stages and became a builder, first of houses and then of office complexes for insurance companies which were in a growth spurt.

His father, my grandpa Florian, was a grape farmer in Fredonia, New York, near Lake Erie. He kept track of time by getting up at the first crack of dawn and walking around his vineyards, intuiting what needed to be done, attending to nuances of soil, weather, plants, and seasons.

He was a strong, compact man with thick wavy white hair, a ruddy complexion, and a peaceful, kindly demeanor. He always smelled fresh and clean, like laundry dried in the sun. He was vigorous until his last days when, aged eighty-seven, he had a stroke and died in his sleep.

His large bright office adjoined one side of the farmhouse. There was a big roll-top desk with lots of cubicles, a wall of glass-doored bookshelves with volumes of farming and town statistics, and a metal office desk with chairs in front of it for people who came to meet with him. Although he had not gone beyond elementary school, he was repeatedly elected town supervisor and served on the school board. He always wore a suit and tie.

I never knew my paternal grandma. She died in her sleep two years before I was born. I was given her middle name, Elizabeth, as a middle name. She appeared to my father at the foot of his death bed and welcomed him to the other side. In a dream she gave me two roses which I took to prophesy my daughters.

In 1968 my aunt prepared a book of five generations of my father's family beginning with my great-great-grandparents. They were born at the beginning of the 19th century, just before the industrial revolution broke through in Germany with production of coal, steel, and railroads. They were the parents of my great-grandparents, the generation that left German-speaking areas in Europe in the mid-19th century. Her account ends with my generation, to which I can now add my children and grandchildren, a seventh generation.

As is traditional from the Bible, she recorded the generations by the father line, each familial generation averaging twenty to thirty years. These seven generations correspond to a period of rapid change in our lifeways. We now also classify people by social generations that are increasingly of fewer years than family generations. The Silent Generation (my generation) and the Boomers are each less than twenty years. Gen X, Y, and Z are accounted as about fifteen years each.

Now there are genealogical DNA tests to recover the separate journeys of our mother and father lines out of Africa. The Ur-mother, the origin of our human mitochondrial DNA lineage, carried by both men and women, lived around 150,000 years ago. The Ur-father, the origin of the human Y-chromosome lineage, carried only by men, lived around 200,000-300,000 years ago. My mitochondrial test tracked how my foremothers wandered north through the middle east and all the way up to northern Scandinavia before they got to Germany. Thinking of so many foreparents makes me want to honor their efforts with care for the generations to come, "caring today for seven generations of tomorrow," as I'm reminded by my recycled tissue wrapper.

Beginning around the new millennium, my college students increasingly complained of stress and anxiety. To help them alleviate their stress, I developed courses that included the theory and practice of meditation and contemplative arts.

Over the last ten or so years, ever more attached to their cellphones, the internet, and virtual reality, they became decreasingly responsive to non-virtual lived experience. As I read in Jonathan Haidt's *The Anxious Generation* (2024), this phenomenon is characteristic of Gen Z, people born between 1997 and 2012. They never knew a world without cellphones and internet, gaming, and social media. Virtual education during covid, the rise of AI, the pressures of social media, and the commodification of attention have reprogrammed their young brains and nervous systems.

It may be that the rapid escalation of global warming, of glaciers melting, of species dying, with the time scale of these predicted disasters shortening year by year, is so disturbing for their generation that they bury themselves in virtual reality as something over which they have at least superficial control with their digits. They will experience all this feared doom more than we who are old and who failed to reverse it. The dangers are unbearably real, quantitatively factual, and non-virtual.

Almost a quarter of their generation identify as LGBTQ+, compared with 14% of Millennials and less than five percent of the previous social generations. Two of my three Gen Z grandchildren are trans. They also suffer from inherited mental and physical health and neurodivergent issues including ADHD, which has made school difficult for three of my grandchildren. Diagnoses of ADHD have increased in their generation, leading to retrospective identification in previous generations, including in Marty, their father, whose father line is Ojibway.

The family now lives on Madeline Island in Lake Superior, an island sacred to the Ojibway. Marty jokes that it is "two and a half miles from the rest of the world." He has become trained as a fire fighter and emergency responder, channeling his attention and hyperactivity to good purpose. The island is subject to Canadian wildfire smoke, heat domes, and the irregularities of climate change, but the surrounding waters are beautiful. They are so deep that, even in storms, the island feels peaceful. It is the world's largest freshwater lake.

In this family's story there is cross-generational historical trauma. Marty's Ojibway grandfather Eddie was of a generation that was put in Indian boarding schools and cut off from ancestral land, family, language, and culture. As an adult, he worked for the auto industry in Michigan and fell prey to alcohol. His son Lester, Marty's father, fell prey to alcohol, drugs, and mental illness and became a ward of state. As a small child Marty was taken from his parents, put in foster care, and adopted. As an adult, he too fell prey to alcohol, then in his late twenties committed himself to sobriety. He reconnected with Eddie and Lester and took care of them to the end of their days. His son, my grandson Ivan, also fell prey to alcohol in his teens. He committed to sobriety in his early twenties.

Ivan is a movingly deep, spiritual, and thoughtful person. He has a patient appreciation of slow process, of taking time over whatever he does. He thrives on such traditional time-consuming practices as making birchbark baskets, harvesting wild rice in canoes, and working with stones, coming to know their different qualities. He gravitates toward activities that involve danger if his attention lapses. For example, he works as a roofer and he has become skillful at flintknapping and mushrooming.

In his commitment to doing and teaching Indigenous craft traditions, he embodies a teaching of Edward Benton-Banai's *The Mishomis Book: The Voice of the Ojibway* (1988), written for First Nations people who have lost the teachings of their elders. In contrast to the road to technology, "the road to spirituality represents the slower path that traditional Native people have traveled and are now seeking again. The Earth is not scorched on this trail....If we natural people of the Earth could just wear the face of brotherhood [with all living things], we might be able to deliver our society from the road to destruction." This teaching comes at the end of a series of seven prophecies of seven "fires," times or stages in the abandonment of old ways, with loss of the language and wisdom of elders, as Ojibway fall prey to the "Light-Skinned" people's dominance.

Indeed, we "Light-Skinned" too fall prey to our destructive dominance. I listened to an Ezra Klein conversation with Kyla Scanlon on "How the Attention Economy Is Devouring Gen Z – and the Rest of Us." Daily emails alone draw my attention to more environmental, social, and political crises, all important to know about, than I can meaningfully process or address, to say nothing about the constant deluge of junk email. When I see Gen Z people like Ivan who are alive and in the living world in their own wonderful, surprising, unique way and not being devoured, I inherit for a moment my father's trust that this world, a world I care about, will go on.

My youngest granddaughter Zoe is also not being devoured. Her generation is Alpha, a new beginning. At fourteen, among her extracurriculars, she has learned survival skills at Wild Earth summer camp, is a "fungal associate" of Completely Arbortrary committed to the love and knowledge of trees, reads long novels, and participates in the Hudson River Eel Project's counting and releasing of young glass eels as they migrate upstream in rivers where they live for years before returning a thousand miles to the Sargasso Sea from which they came. There they will create the next generation.

2.

In a *New York Times* guest essay, "Why Gen Z Is Resurrecting the 1990s," Clay Routledge reports that 80% of Gen Z adults are concerned that their generation is over-dependent on tech, 75% worry about the impact of social media on young people's mental health, and 68% feel nostalgia for times before their lifetime.

Routledge is a social psychologist specializing in the benefits of historical nostalgia for enriching the present and future. He differentiates this from romantic nostalgia, a kind of sentimental melancholy, and from nostalgia as a persuasive political tool. I hadn't realized that nostalgia has been found to have observable positive psychological functions such as cultivating social and cultural connectedness and meaning.

This kind of active nostalgia sounds particularly relevant to environmental restoration. Ivan is an excellent example. His partner, in her study and application of traditional Indigenous farming techniques to regenerative farming, is another example.

Perhaps it is a form of nostalgia that I like long novels set in interesting historical contexts with a focus on culture, often with a narrator's perspective from a later time and a protagonist's consciousness of changing times.

The novel I have reread most often is Hermann Hesse's *The Glass Bead Game.* I am drawn to its focus on education and the way it integrates scholarly history and contemplation, study and practice, self-realization and ethical community. I, like Hesse and his protagonist, have felt tension in these polarities and practice meditative techniques for their appeasement while remaining invested in a polarized world.

Hesse develops the story under the guise of a 2400 CE chronicler composing a biography set two centuries before his, two centuries after ours. It is introduced "for the layman" by a discussion of materialism and spiritual degeneration from the 19th to the mid-21st century, a period including my lifetime. We learn the history of the Game and how, for each player, it "is primarily a form of music-making." It is grounded in the study and practice of pre-romantic European music 1500-1800, particularly Bach, whose fugal keyboard music I have amateurly studied and play along with other Baroque music and Haydn and Mozart sonatas.

One of my favorite scenes is early in the biography. The young protagonist Joseph has his first music lesson with the old Music Master, who plays him a fugue. With devotion, Joseph senses "the world of Spirit/Mind (*Geist*) behind the music being created in his presence, the joy-giving harmony of law and freedom, of service and rule." The Master tells him, "Our mission is to recognize contraries for what they are: first as contraries, but then as opposite poles of a unity....These antinomies...are subjective, not objective."

This insight, this fugal mystery of the Game transmitted to Joseph by the Music Master, shapes the novel. This is also what life, through all its complexities, continually teaches me and what I continually learn and remember in a new way, including every time I reread the novel.

Hesse was fifty when he started this book project in 1927. It began as a series of biographies with a single protagonist reincarnating in different historical epochs. Reincarnation was a way to affirm his sense of a continuous spiritual and intellectual quest underlying the flux of time. By 1933, the biography of Joseph Knecht, the Master of the Game, took predominance, with the other biographies appended as Joseph's posthumous writings.

According to Hesse's biographer Joseph Mileck, Hesse's choice of the name Joseph was influenced by his appreciation of Thomas Mann's *Tales of Jacob,* the first novel in Mann's *Joseph and his Brothers* tetralogy. The tetralogy has recently replaced Mann's *Magic Mountain* as my favorite novel. *Glass Bead Game* and the tetralogy were their authors' personally stabilizing projects during the era when Nazism took over their country. They corresponded with one another in exile. The Hesse biographer Gunnar Decker discusses their shared sense of an "urgent need for a protected space beyond the clutches of barbarity," their concern about future generations and the survival of civilized values, a sense and concern so many of us share today.

After reading *Tales of Jacob,* Hesse wrote to Mann, "Given the modern conception of history and historiography, I have naturally grown very fond, right down to the tiniest detail, of that quiet, gently melancholic form of irony with which you ultimately treat the problem of all history and every desire to recount stories, without for a moment relinquishing your own efforts to write the sort of historiography that you have recognized is fundamentally impossible."

Like Serenus Zeitblom, Mann's narrator in *Doktor Faustus,* also written during the Nazi period, and like his tetralogy narrator, a self-consciously modern voice writing about a legendary Biblical time millenia ago, Hesse's chronicler has his own mock pedantic version of a "quiet, gently melancholic form of irony." He repeatedly acknowledges that his knowledge is limited and the story is complicated. He sticks as close as possible to what can be supported by evidence.

Hesse articulates the novel's view of history through the Benedictine historian Father Jacobus, a character based on the Swiss cultural historian Jacob Burckhardt. Joseph admires in Jacobus his "wonderful note of equivocation, ranging through the whole compass from earnestness to irony," a note he also appreciates in Thomas von der Trave, his predecessor as Master of the Game, a character based on Thomas Mann. When Joseph writes his circular letter of resignation as Master of the Game, having decided to become an ordinary teacher, he/Hesse appends a remark he noted down from a private lesson with Father Jacobus. Mileck points out that the remark is a direct quote from Burckhardt's fragment *The Age of Revolution*: "Times of terror and deepest misery may be in the offing. But if any happiness at all is to be extracted from that misery, it can be only a spiritual happiness, looking backward toward the conservation of the culture of earlier times, looking forward toward serene and stalwart defense of the things of the spirit in an age which otherwise might succumb wholly to material things."

Burckhardt/Jacobus confirmed for Hesse/Joseph that the spirit is continuous but mutable. Spiritual order and meaning can be lost through institutional decay, cultural collapse, and the chaos of temporal reality, but they reappear in a new way. Burckhardt portrays historical examples of this continuum in his classic companion books *Constantine the Great* (1852) and *The Civilization of the Renaissance in Italy* (1860). In the first book, the "crisis" and "senescence" of classical culture give way to medieval other-worldliness. In the second book, the medieval gives way to a rise of worldliness and revival of antiquity.

The Civilization of the Renaissance in Italy concludes with a consideration of the Florentine Platonic Academy, the primary subject of my graduate school mentor Professor Kristeller's scholarship. Burckhardt writes of his admiration for the Platonic hymns of Lorenzo il Magnifico. They set forth "a theism which strives to treat the world as a great moral and physical cosmos." In contrast to others' other-worldly religious preoccupations, "the doctrine is upheld that the visible world was created by God in love, that it is the copy of a pattern pre-existing in Him, and that He will ever remain its ethical mover and restorer." Burckhardt considers this "one of the most precious fruits of the knowledge of the world and of man."

Joseph meets Jacobus where he lives in Mariafels, a Christian monastery in the "great other world" outside of Castalia, the sequestered province of the Game. Joseph has been given the task of developing a relationship and dialogue between the monastery and Castalia. Jacobus critiques the abstract mathematical design of the Game as shallowly elite, lacking in human reality, in good and evil, in history, in time past and future, in moral responsibility to the larger community. He tells Joseph, "To study history means submitting to chaos and nevertheless retaining faith in order and meaning. It is a very serious task, young man, and possibly a tragic one."

In Hesse's novel, Joseph comes to feel, after the death of the Music Master, a similar love, gratitude, and reverence for Father Jacobus. It is an affection Hesse came to feel for Burckhardt as a moral corrective to his own aestheticism as a young man.

Hesse rejected Buddhist and Indian spiritualities as too ascetic and life-denying, not sufficiently individualistic. His character Siddhartha learns from life and the river, not Buddha. Hesse preferred the Chinese classics for their worldly applications, especially the *I Ching or Book of Changes,* available since 1924 in Richard Wilhelm's German translation. In the novel, the Elder Brother introduces Joseph to the I Ching's oracle game played with yarrow stalks, a meditation game Hesse practiced. In his introduction, Wilhelm points out that manipulation of the yarrow sticks "requires a clear and tranquil mind, receptive to the cosmic influences hidden in the humble divining sticks. As products of the vegetable kingdom, these were considered to be related to the sources of life."

The theme of the I Ching is the natural and social dynamics of change, the complementary relationships of opposites, and the underlying oneness as reflected in the clear and tranquil mind contemplating and playing, as an individual player, in harmony with the shifting patterns. In the Elder Brother's bamboo grove hermitage, Joseph sits by its goldfish pool and gazes "into the cool small world of darkness and light and magically shimmering colors." The image intimates the tai chi circle of duality, interdependence, and balance.

Seeking seclusion, contemplation, and to continue his Chinese studies, he has journeyed here southward through the mountains. According to Hesse's biographer Mileck, the natural beauty, peace, and culture of the hermitage represents Hesse's idyllic retreat in Montagnola, where he lived from 1919 to his death in 1962, including while writing *The Glass Bead Game,* and where he cultivated a bamboo grove. Hesse found this way to incorporate a nuance of eastern contemplative culture into the predominately western matrix of Joseph's education and his own life.

In 1946 he was awarded the Nobel prize for this novel, certifying him as master of his game. Thomas Mann, who recommended him for the prize, said of *The Glass Bead Game,* "This chaste and daring work...raises the intimate and familiar to a new intellectual, yes, revolutionary level...It belongs to the highest and purist spiritual aspirations and labors of our epoch."

During the seventeen years Hesse lived after the war, he wrote no more novels or short stories and few poems. Like the Elder Brother, he followed a semi-reclusive daily ritual of writing, reading, watercolor painting, gardening, correspondence, music, and receiving guests from time to time. My similar daily ritual has perhaps been unconsciously shaped by my frequent rereadings of this book.

3.

It is October 10, 2025. I am keeping too much track of time. Today is Trump's 263rd day in office. The government has been shut down since October 1. During Trump's previous term, there was a record shutdown for 35 days. At this moment there are 1197 days, 16 hours, 34 minutes, and 46 seconds until his reign ends on January 20, 2029. By then I will either be 88 years old or departed from this history.

With my daughter and granddaughter, I plan to attend a No Kings rally next Saturday. I just began a subscription to *The Nation*. Mann's *Joseph* tetralogy continues to be my daily escape from the Here and Now. One of its themes is the relation between time and timelessness, between unique particulars and perennial mythic patterns of dying and rising.

In *The Ironic German: A Study of Thomas Mann* (1958) chapter on "The Theology of Irony," Erich Heller describes the tension between the singular and the universal as a "leitmotif of Mann's mind." Relationships between dualities are also a preoccupation of my mind. This may be a mental characteristic of Geminis. (I was born on June 4 and he was born on June 6.)

I have reached the part of *Joseph the Provider,* the last volume in the tetralogy, where Joseph, now thirty years old, is brought before Pharaoh Amenhotep IV to interpret Pharaoh's dream. This is the Pharaoh, aka Akhenaton (1351-1334 B.C.), famed for his failed monotheistic reform of ancient Egypt's traditional polytheism, an innovative reform based on his spiritual passion for his god Aten, symbolized by a sun disc. (Akhenaton is not mentioned in the Biblical source of Joseph's story.)

Already in the previous volume, *Joseph in Egypt,* there was tension between traditional and innovative views of religion and culture. Joseph, a Hebrew, an articulate foreign thinker, has come into favor with progressive members of Pharaoh's court. In Mann's telling, a traditional conservative priest is determined to get rid of him. Influenced by the priest's faction, the wife of the liberal courtier Potiphar falsely accuses Joseph of sexually assaulting her. As in scripture, she has sought and failed to seduce him. Her charge forces Potiphar to send him to prison.

Akhenaton's conventional dream interpreters and learned wise men have not been able to elucidate his dream for him. A courtier reports his experience of Joseph's ability to correctly interpret dreams. On his recommendation, Joseph is brought from prison to the court.

Akhenaton asks Joseph if he, like a prophet, will enter a wild trance state when his God gives him the interpretation of the dream. Joseph says, no, his manner is composed and reasonable. He associates both reason and unique particulars with God.

Joseph's explanation incapsulates the way the time/timelessness motif has evolved, from its appearances in Mann's earlier works, to what Heller describes as his "most daringly humorous and most 'baroque' treatment." One of the characteristics of baroque art is the juxtaposition of contrasting metaphysical elements, especially the intimate incommensurability of man and God.

Joseph says, "It is an I and a single individual through whom the typical and the traditional are being fulfilled, and thereby, in my feeling, the seal of divine reason is vouchsafed to them. For the pattern and the traditional come from the depths which lie beneath and are what binds us, whereas the I is from God and is of the Spirit, which is free. But what constitutes civilized life is that the binding and the traditional depth shall fulfil itself in the freedom of God which belongs to the I; there is no human civilization without the one and without the other."

When I read that in the novel, I fell into wordless appreciation and lost all track of time. My Buddhist views failed to chatter at Joseph's intimately personal theology.

Joseph has twice been cast into the depths, out of the comforts of his civilized life, each time maturing his sense of himself, his awareness of deep patterns, and his trust in the God of his fathers. His words do not imply that his realization is based on a mystical experience beyond words, received in a self-consuming rapture. It carries the seal of divine reason, aka logos, and communicates through language.

Joseph's inherited story of Abraham's friendship with God appears in *Young Joseph,* the second novel in the tetralogy. "God was present, and Abraham walked before Him.... They were two, an I and a Thou, both of whom said 'I' to the other 'Thou.'... God was also in Abraham who, through his own strength of mind and soul, had discovered Him....It was on this foundation that God made His covenant with Abraham."

In "The Theology of Irony," Heller identifies Angelus Silesius's 17th-century German mystical work *The Cherubinic Wanderer* as the predominate source of Mann's version of Joseph's spiritual legacy from Abraham. Silesius's work consists mostly of two-line epigrams in the tradition of previous German mystics, particularly Jakob Boehme and Meister Eckhart. Over the years I have gone through periods of studying and connecting with these mystics, as well as with English 17th-century baroque metaphysical poetry, the province of my late husband. Meister Eckhart's most well-known saying, declared heretical in his time, is "the eye with which I see God is the same as the eye with which God sees me."

Heller writes, "It would be possible to quote for almost every sentence of Thomas Mann's chapter [on Abraham and God] a couplet from *Der Cherubinische Wandersmann.* "Here are three examples of epigrams on the I, God, time, and timelessness.

I am eternity when I leave time
and join myself in God and God in me. (I.13)

Time is like eternity, eternity like time,
unless between them I draw a line. (I.47)

God cares as much for me as I for Him:
I help as much to guard His Being as He guards mine. (I.100)

Heller points out that Mann shapes Akhenaton's theological realizations to correspond to those of Abraham, so that they too are touched by German mysticism. For example, after Joseph has drawn from Pharaoh the interpretation of his dream, Pharaoh says to Joseph, "Our being is only the meeting-place between not-being and ever-being; our temporal only the medium of the eternal. ...we must ask ... Which bestows more worth: the Eternal upon the Here and Now, the Unique and Particular, or the Here and Now upon the Eternal? It is a beautiful question, one of those to which there is no answer."

At this point Pharaoh's mother, who has been his regent until he recently came of age, chides him for getting lost "in the most remote and impossible speculations" and "extravagant abstractions" while the dream's prediction of seven fat years followed by seven lean years requires immediate practical attention. Unlike Pharaoh, Pharaoh's mother and Joseph have a sense that civilization requires individual work and timely action as well as deep patterns, a reminder for me to return to the present, which at this moment involves putting bread in the oven.

Moderation

I have observed in myself with age
a moderation of drama.
Possibly there is endocrinal fatigue
from high-adrenaline years.
When I was young with juices to spare
I thrilled at emitting them.
Now I am more abstemious, inclined
to a steady state,
not bored by that. Amidst rhythms of change,
I slow down.
Sometimes in this slowing with less melancholy
griefs become meditations.
Perhaps time has settled the fear of their anguish.
Perhaps, more alone,
I feel sorrow as a form of communion.

A Guru in the Form of a Woman

The last teaching I attended with Khenpo Karthar Rinpoche before his passing in October 2019 was on a classic text by Shantideva on the way of compassion. We students were moved to see him weep as he read, his tears watering the text he was teaching. During Q&A a student asked why he was crying. We assumed there was some pain or sorrow. Maybe there were health issues from old age (he was ninety-five). He said, "I was so happy, so grateful to Shantidev for giving us this treasure to keep in our hearts."

He was devoted to the practice of White Tara, Mother of Buddhas. From the deep space of wisdom, through skillful means, her female form manifests with maternal compassion in action to relax harmful forces within us destructive of long life with well-being. He visualized her as the color of the moon, peaceful and smiling, radiating five colors.

Shortly after his death, his teaching center KTD closed because of covid. When it reopened in October 2022, I went to a teaching and empowerment to begin a preliminary practice of Chöd, a method for pacifying physical and mental demons. The practice was initiated by Machik Lapdrön, a Tibetan woman seen as an incarnation of Tara and Prajña (Perfect Wisdom, Mother of Buddhas). Her life spanned ninety-nine years from the middle of the 11th to the middle of the 12th century. She composed dharma teachings addressing the particular needs of individual students and transmitted her teachings to her two sons Tönyön and Drubpa, her four spiritual daughters, and many others across all Tibet. Through practices she prescribed, her son Tönyön overcame severe mental illness. Drubpa's great granddaughter Lentokma was considered an aspect of Machik's emanation of Tara and Prajña and spread her teachings.

I found myself unexpectedly connecting to her Chöd practice. One of my fellow students told me how he began doing it twenty years ago as he battled cancer and HIV. It helped him win those battles. Now he also applies the practice to cutting through the demons of others, their diseases, their addictions, exchanging self and other, feeding the demons.

At the time my daughter was fighting Stage IV breast cancer. I had recently finished surgery and radiation for Stage I breast cancer and anticipated on-going gerontological concerns. My two trans grandchildren were struggling with social, mental, and physical health issues.

I began to study Sarah Harding's translation of *Machik's Complete Explanation: Clarifying the Meaning of Chöd* (2003), I added the practice to my bedtime ritual. Since Machik's teachings are rooted in the Prajñaparamita Sutras, I added an image of Prajña to my evening prayer table, along with Machik and White Tara.

More than fifty years ago, when my mother was dying and my father and sister-in-law had recently died, I connected to an old Sanskrit liturgy, *Devi Mahatmyam*, that tells stories of the Mother Goddess killing various demons of injustice. She became my chosen deity for deity yoga practice. Machik, Tara, and Prajña represent, for me, a Tibetan Buddhist modification and continuation of that focus on a maternal/female rather than a paternal/male deity image.

Tibetan prayer liturgies and devotional visualizations integrate traditions from India and from Bön, an indigenous Tibetan shamanic tradition. I like to feel how these traditions developed from ancient indigenous spiritual practices with ritual arts interconnecting all the phenomena of life, the earth, the sky, and the cosmos into wholeness, bringing about balance and well-being at all levels. Prayer in song or chant, usually involving repetition and a small number of pitches, becomes a harmonic weave or web, bringing mind, body, and world into tune. The songlines of Australian Aborigines are perhaps the most well-known and most ancient surviving example of this practice. Hermann Hesse's *The Glass Bead Game,* grounded in music, is an imaginative modern adaptation. Tibetan mandalas have parallels in Native American medicine wheels and Navajo ritual art. Their practice cultivates an attitude of gratitude, devotion, humility, and service within circles of interconnection both intimate and vast. Their aura feels ecological, natural, contemplative, and peaceful, rebalancing aggressive, invasive, and harmful imbalances in my mind and its relationship with the world.

Today China occupies Machik's land of Tibet. Her culture and language are endangered. The teachings come to us through translators and teachers in exile. In the wild places where she meditated, climate change melts snowcaps blackened by sooty rains. Dams control the life of Asia's nine great rivers sourced there: Indus, Sutlej, Ganges, Brahmaputra, Irrawaddy, Salween, Mekong, Yangtse, and Yellow.

Where I am on the other side of the world, pipelines, bomb trains, tankers, mines, and drills create spills poisoning waters and all living beings that depend upon water. Everywhere we humans are collectively and individually occupied, tainted, and blocked by our demons, in opposition with nature and one another as we face myriad crises.

Machik's word translated as demon is *mara,* from a Sanskrit root verb meaning to die or obstruct (physically, mentally, or spiritually). In Buddha's life story, Mara the Tempter repeatedly tries and fails to provoke in him the root poisons of desire, aggression, and ignorance, much as Satan tried to provoke Jesus in the wilderness. Machik developed precise analyses of these obstructions and how to cut through them. Her *Complete Explanation* is full of vivid physical and mental detail. I think of this as in keeping with a woman's tendency to integrate the physical and mental sides of her experience in practical ways, to not err on the side of abstraction.

For confronting our demons, Machik tells us, "Relax. Do not be anxious. Do not be the least bit anxious." She voices the wisdom and compassion of a mother elder who has come to know all the thoughts and emotions that arise and subside in minds, including those particular to a woman growing old, and to let them go.

Resting the Mind

My mother used to savor each day's end.
She felt she went downhill after ten in the morning.
She looked forward to putting on her nightgown.

Waking before dawn, she sat in a blue wing-back chair, drank coffee,
and rested her gaze on the changing nuances of crab tree boughs
as they came into view on the other side of the window.

Perhaps through quiet prayer she discovered on her own
this way of resting her mind which was restless by nature,
concerned with justice, prone to argument, ready for action.

Willena Hope was her name. (Her parents hoped for William.)
I detect some inner Willie in myself and my daughters
as we sit in our morning chairs and make ready for a new day.

Endnotes

—Transience

C. G. Sebald, *A Place in the Country* (2013)

—Books, Seeds, and Stars

Daniel Arasse. *Anselm Kiefer* (2015)

Michael Auping, *Anselm Kiefer: Heaven and Earth* (2005)

—Aging with Lucretius, Venus, and Buddha

Lucretius, Martin Ferguson Smith, tr., *On the Nature of Things* (2001)

David Farrell Kroll, *The Death of Empedocles* (2008)

Michael Hamburger, *Hölderlin Poems and Fragments* (2004)

M. R. Wright, *Empedocles: Extant Fragments* (1995)

Therigatha, Charles Hallisey, tr. (2014)

—Subtle Wanderings

Richard Ellmann, *Yeats: the Man and the Mask* (1948)

Aldous Huxley, *The Perennial Philosophy* (1945)

—History and the Moon

Hermann Kurzke, *Mondwanderungen: Wegweiser durch Thomas Manns Joseph-Roman* (1993)

J. J. Bachofen, *Myth, Religion, and Mother Right: Selected Writings* (1967)

—The Horizontal and the Vertical

Barnett Newman: Selected Writings and Interviews (1990)

John Golding, *Paths to the Absolute* (2000)

Ann Temkin, *Barnett Newman* (2002)

Maurice Tuchman, *The Spiritual in Art* (1987)

Leesa Fanning, *Encountering the Spiritual in Contemporary Art* (2018)

Norbert Wolff, *Caspar David Friedrich: The Painter of Stillness* (2007)

—The Shape of My Shadow
Robert A. Birmingham & Leslie E. Eisenberg, *Indian Mounds of Wisconsin* (2000)

—Keeping and Losing Track of Time
Joseph Mileck, *Hermann Hesse: Life and Art* (1978)
Gunnar Decker, *Hesse: The Wanderer and His Shadow* (2018)

Biographical Notes

Suzanne Ironbiter is a retired teacher of Philosophy and Humanistic Studies with a doctorate in Religion. This collection is the third in a series of five-year books that began when she, as a way of reorienting toward old age upon turning seventy, took Buddhist refuge and the bodhisattva vow. Whereas her previous writing developed from her mythopoetic contemplations and studies in mysticism, her five-year books are affected by her engagement with Buddhist theory and practice.

Catherine Ednie is a retired software consultant with keen interests in plants, fiber arts, and bookmaking. She gravitated toward a more analog way of life after moving from Connecticut to coastal Maine in 2016. A lot of her projects are based on collaboration with local plants to make botanical prints and dyes.

www.ingramcontent.com/pod-product-compliance
Lightning Source LLC
LaVergne TN
LVHW051000080826
845145LV00009B/2385
* 9 7 8 0 9 9 7 6 2 1 8 5 3 *